500

cookies

500
cookies

philippa vanstone

APPLE

A Quintet Book

Published by Apple Press
7 Greenland Street
London NW1 0ND
United Kingdom

www.apple-press.com

ISBN: 978-1-84543-073-3

This book was designed and produced by
Quintet Publishing Limited
6 Blundell Street
London N7 9BH

Project Editor: Jenny Doubt
Editor: Ruth Patrick
Art Director: Roland Codd
Photography: Ian Garlick
Stylist: Susannah Blake
Home Economist: Fergal Connelly
Publisher: Ian Castello-Cortes

10 9 8 7 6 5

Manufactured in Singapore by Pica Digital Pte Ltd.
Printed in China by Toppan Leefung Printing International Ltd.

contents

introduction	6
classic cookies	18
teatime cookies	54
cookies for kids	90
chocolate cookies	126
celebration cookies	160
wholesome cookies	194
cookies for special diets	228
cookie bars	254
dessert cookies	286
savoury cookies & crackers	324
index	356

introduction

Susannah Blake

The modern-day cookie is said to be an American invention, although versions of these sweet confections can be found throughout the world, with every country boasting its own speciality. The earliest cookies can be traced back centuries – the Romans made a cookie consisting of a pasta-like dough that was fried and served with honey, while other cookies have been traced back to 7th-century Persia, one of the first countries to cultivate sugar.

The term 'cookie' was first used in the United States, and is derived from the Dutch word *koekje* which signifies the little cakes that were brought to New York by early settlers. However, generations of immigrants from Germany, Eastern Europe, Scandinavia, England, Scotland and Ireland have also made their mark on the history of the cookie.

the earliest cookies

The largely British term 'biscuit' is derived from the Latin *panis biscoctus*, meaning 'bread twice-cooked'. These savoury Roman biscuits were baked twice to dry them out, giving them a longer life, thus making them ideal for feeding armies and travellers. Sweet cookies such as German *zwieback*, Jewish *Mandelbrot*, and Italian *biscotti* and *cantucci*, which are all twice-baked, undoubtedly evolved from these early biscuits.

Pretzels date back as far as C.E. 610. They were invented by monks in a monastery in France, where they were used to symbolise the marriage bond. The twisted strands of dough are furthermore said to symbolise a child's arms folded in prayer; the holes the Holy Trinity.

Gingerbread is thought to have been first baked in Europe at the end of the 11th century, after crusaders introduced the spicy ginger root. It then became a speciality of medieval Germany, and by the 17th century gingerbread baking was recognised as a profession –

only professional gingerbread makers were permitted to bake the spicy confection in both Germany and France. It was also in medieval Germany that the tradition of crafting cookie dough into shapes at Christmas became a tradition. However, the first gingerbread 'men' are credited to the court of Elizabeth I of England, where important visitors were favoured with gingerbread likenesses of themselves. Gingerbread houses first appeared in Germany in the early 19th century after the brothers Grimm published their first collection of fairytales, including the story of Hansel and Gretel.

Recipes for shortbread and shortcake have been popular since the 16th century. Petticoat tails, the classic shortbread baked in a round and marked into wedges, resembles a crinoline petticoat and is thought to date back to the 12th century. The American butter cookie bears a strong resemblance to this traditional shortbread.

Cookies made of whisked egg whites and ground nuts have been popular since the Middle Ages, and gave rise to macaroon-type cookies. Furthermore, the discovery that beaten egg aerated cookie mixtures giving a lighter texture, led to the evolution of sponge biscuits, boudoir biscuits, Lisbon biscuits and Naples biscuits and jumbles.

During the 19th century sugar, flour and chemical raising agents such as bicarbonate of soda became readily available and affordable, leading to the development of many sweet cookie recipes. Industrialisation then made the manufacture of cookies in factories possible, beckoning in the era of mass-produced cookies. Cookies today are found in tiny, bite-size shapes, as traybakes cut into squares and bars, or as giant cookies that are served like cake; they can be served plain, dusted with sugar, coated in chocolate, spread with icing, drizzled with glaze, decorated with sweets or sandwiched with a rich creamy filling. Whatever your taste, you'll find them all here to bake, sample and serve — straight from your kitchen.

advice for readers

how to use this book
Each of the chapters in this book is comprised of two sections: a series of base recipes and a number of variations on each of the base recipes – with a slight modification of the original recipe, the addition of a cup of raisins or substitution of melted chocolate for white chocolate chips for example, you can create a host of new and exciting cookies.

wrapping, serving & storing
We have suggested that parchment paper be used to wrap dough and line standard baking trays where a non-stick baking tray is not available. Cling film can also be used to wrap dough that requires refrigerating. Foil is recommended for dough that needs to be wrapped and refrigerated in a specific shape. Serving and storage information is indicated at the end of each recipe – though please note that these are only approximates.

sugar, eggs & chocolate
Unless the recipe indicates that eggs should be beaten, combine them into the recipe whole. When recipes call for brown sugar, ensure that you pack the sugar when measuring it out in order that the correct amount is used. Finally, we recommend that unrefined sugar be used in recipes contained in the Wholesome chapter, as this chapter is comprised of recipes whose ingredients and preparations offer healthier options. Replace dark and milk chocolate according to taste.

refrigerated vs fresh dough
If cooking from refrigerated dough, preheat the oven to the temperature indicated 15 minutes before you want to bake the prepared cookie dough.

equipment

You need only a few basic pieces of equipment to make most cookies.

scales, measuring jugs & spoons
Baking is an exact science, so correct measuring equipment is essential. If the proportions of ingredients are incorrect the cookies may not work, so always use accurate weighing scales, calibrated measuring jugs and proper measuring spoons.

mixing bowls & spoons
You will need a large bowl and wooden spoon for mixing most doughs. Small-sized bowls are useful for melting butter or chocolate or for mixing small quantities such as frosting. A large metal spoon is useful for folding ingredients into delicate mixtures.

sieves
You will need a large sieve for sifting dry ingredients such as flour and a small sieve for dusting icing sugar or cocoa over baked cookies.

rolling pin
Useful for making rolled cookies, although you can use a straight-sided bottle instead. Mini rolling pins are easy for children to use.

cookie cutters
You can cut out rolled cookie dough by hand using a sharp knife, though it's much easier to use cookie cutters. They are available in all shapes and sizes, including rounds, hearts, stars and Christmas trees.

baking sheets & trays

Most cookies are best baked on a flat baking sheet. Baking trays, which have a lip around all four sides, can be used as well, but the flat shape of the sheet allows air to more effectively circulate around the cookie.

palette knives & metal spatulas

Useful for transferring uncooked rolled cookies onto baking sheets, or transferring baked cookies to a wire rack. Small palette knives are good for spreading cookies with filling or icing.

timers

When baking cookies, timing is crucial, so it's advisable to always use a timer. Accurate digital timers are inexpensive and well worth the investment.

wire racks

After baking, most cookies should be transferred to a wire rack to cool.

other equipment

Electric mixers can be great time-savers for mixing cookie doughs – these can be bought quite cheaply as well. A whisk is essential for whisking egg whites and helpful for removing lumps from mixtures. Marble pastry boards can be useful for rolling out cookie dough. Piping bags and nozzles are useful for making piped cookies as well as for decorating baked cookies. For piping icing and melted chocolate, you can usually use a small plastic bag with the corner snipped off. A pastry brush is useful for brushing glazes on to unbaked or baked cookies.

ingredients

Most cookies are made using three basic ingredients: butter, sugar and flour with the frequent addition of other ingredients such as eggs, chocolate, nuts and vanilla.

butter & other fats
Unsalted butter is usually best for cookie-making. For rubbed-in cookie mixtures use cold, firm butter; for creamed mixtures, use butter at room temperature; for melted mixtures, dice the butter before gently warming. Margarine, white cooking fats and mild-tasting vegetable oils are sometimes used instead of butter and are a good choice for those with a dairy intolerance or allergy.

sugar & other sweeteners
There are many different types of sugar, all of which add their own unique taste and texture to cookies. Refined white sugars add sweetness, while unrefined brown sugars add flavour. The texture of the sugar will also affect the cookie. Caster sugar is most frequently used for cookie-making, but granulated sugar and coarse-textured sugars such as demerera sugar and moist sugars such as muscovado sugar are also used. Icing sugar is generally used for dusting cookies and making icing.

Light golden syrup, maple syrup, honey and treacle can also be used in cookies, either in place of, or alongside, sugar. They give a distinctive taste and texture and are a frequent addition to melted cookie mixtures.

flour & flour alternatives
Most cookies are made with plain flour or self-raising flour – this gives them a lighter texture. Wholemeal flour is sometimes used, but produces cookies with a heavier,

denser texture. Non-wheat flours, often combined with wheat flour, can also be used. These include cornmeal, oatmeal, cornflour and rice flour. Rolled oats and ground nuts are common alternatives to flour.

eggs
These enrich cookie mixtures and bind ingredients together. For the best results use eggs at room temperature. When whisking egg whites be sure to use a clean, grease-free bowl.

other ingredients & flavourings
Dried fruits such as raisins, sultanas, apricots and cranberries are a popular addition to cookie mixtures. They are naturally sweet, so you may be able to use less sugar in the actual cookie mixture. Different dried fruits are often interchangeable in recipes.

Nuts are another popular addition, either whole, chopped, flaked or ground. They add a nutty taste, texture and bite.

Seeds such as sunflower, sesame and poppy are often stirred into basic cookie doughs, particularly wholesome and savoury cookie doughs.

Chocolate is widely used in cookie-making, usually as a flavouring, but also as a topping and sometimes as a binding ingredient. Unsweetened cocoa powder can be stirred into basic cookie doughs or used to dust baked cookies. Chocolate chips or chocolate chunks can be stirred into mixtures, and plain, milk or white chocolate can be melted and stirred into mixtures or used to coat or decorate baked cookies. There is a wide selection of various qualities of chocolate available on the market.

Other cookie flavourings include spices, herbs, vanilla, coffee, citrus zest, almond essence and orange essence.

making cookies

With all the hundreds of different cookies in the world, there are still only five main types of mixture: creamed, rubbed-in, melted, whisked and all-in-one. These mixtures can then be used to make eight different types of cookie.

Creamed mixtures are made with soft butter beaten with sugar until fluffy, then blended with flour, eggs and other ingredients. Creamed cookies include classic butter cookies.

Rubbed-in mixtures are made with cold, firm butter, which is rubbed into the flour, then bound together with eggs, milk or another liquid. Scottish shortbread is one of the classic cookies made using the rubbed-in method.

Melted mixtures are made of butter melted with sugar or syrup, which is then combined with dry ingredients. Classic melted cookies include flapjacks or gingerbread.

Whisked mixtures are made of whisked eggs and sugar (or a meringue mixture), into which the dry ingredients are folded. Classic whisked cookies include macaroons.

All-in-one mixtures are made by putting all the ingredients in a bowl and beating them together. These cookies can usually be made in a food processor, with any chunky ingredients such as dried fruit and nuts stirred in at the last minute.

drop cookies

Usually made with a soft creamed or all-in-one mixture, drop cookies are made by dropping spoonfuls of cookie mixture onto a greased baking sheet. They may be soft or firm, and are usually thick. Drop cookies can also be made using melted mixtures. The mixture usually spreads out on the baking sheet and results in large, flat, thin, crisp cookies. Melted drop cookies are often pliable when they come out of the oven and may be shaped while still warm, either rolled around a wooden spoon handle to make tubes, draped over a rolling pin to make curls or moulded over a foil-covered orange to make a basket.

rolled cookies

Made with a firm cookie dough that can be rolled out on a floured surface, these cookies may be made with a creamed, melted or rubbed-in mixture, which is usually chilled before rolling out. They're great for making with children, who will enjoy cutting shapes out of the dough using cookie cutters.

Rolled doughs are also great for making into multi-coloured cookies. Divide the dough into two pieces before chilling and knead a few drops of food colouring or 1 tablespoon cocoa powder into half the dough. Chill, then roll out the two different doughs to equal thickness. Using a large cookie cutter, cut out cookies from each sheet of dough and then, using a smaller cutter, cut out the inside of the cookies. Carefully swap over the cookie centres so that each cookie has a different coloured middle.

Alternatively, make spiral-patterned cookies. Brush the sheet of plain rolled dough with egg white and lay the coloured sheet of dough on top. Roll up tightly to make a log, then slice the dough to make swirly cookies.

piped cookies

Usually made with soft creamed mixtures that are soft enough to press through a piping bag, piped cookies may also be made with whisked mixtures. Piping gives them a professional look, and also makes them very quick and easy to shape. Popular shapes include rosettes, swirls and fingers.

shaped cookies

Firm doughs can be shaped by pressing into moulds or baking trays, or by rolling bite-sized pieces of dough into balls or thin fingers. Fingers of dough can then be shaped into twists or knots. Classic moulded cookies include shortbread, for which special moulds are available, while hand-shaped cookies include pretzels and lovers' knots.

bars and traybakes
Increasingly popular and most often based on creamed, rubbed-in or melted mixtures baked in a baking tray, these cookies can vary enormously in shape, size and texture. Usually cut into squares, bars, fingers or wedges, they may be soft and squidgy, sticky and chewy, or firm and crisp. Bars and traybakes may also be layered, perhaps with a cookie base and an indulgent topping. Classic traybakes include brownies, blondies, flapjacks and the multi-layered millionaire's shortbread.

icebox cookies
The dough for these cookies can be stored in the refrigerator for one to two weeks, so you can make a few freshly baked cookies at a time, or just prepare the dough in advance to save time later. The dough is usually firm, made from creamed, rubbed-in or melted mixtures, and may be kept in a container and scooped on to a baking tray or shaped into balls. Alternatively, it may be rolled into a log shape, wrapped in clear film and then sliced into cookies when you're ready to bake it.

no-bake cookies
Rather than baking, these cookies are set by chilling or cooling. Dry ingredients such as broken cookies, breakfast cereal, nuts, dried fruit and marshmallows are stirred into a melted mixture – usually a combination of butter, chocolate and/or syrup – then pressed into a mould or baking tray and cooled until set.

baking, cooling & storing

Different types of cookie need to be baked at different temperatures, so always follow the recipe instructions. Traybakes are usually cooked in a low to moderate oven (between 160°C / 325°F / Gas mark 3 and 180°C / 350°F / Gas mark 4). Drop cookies are usually baked in a moderate oven (about 180°C / 350°F / Gas mark 4) to allow them to spread while they cook. Rolled, piped and freezer cookies are usually cooked in a moderate to hot oven (between 180°C / 350°F / Gas mark 4 and 200°C / 400°F / Gas mark 6). Some cookies such as biscotti and cantucci are baked twice, first as a loaf of dough, which is then sliced and the individual cookies are returned to the oven to crisp up.

Oven temperatures tend to vary from model to model so always check the cookies a couple of minutes before their baking time is up to avoid overcooking. The temperature within the oven can also vary, so move the baking sheets around halfway through cooking to ensure even cooking. Never bake more than two sheets of cookies at a time because it may cause the oven temperature to drop.

Cookies baked on a baking sheet should usually be left to firm up for a few minutes, before transferring to a wire rack to cool. This allows air to circulate around the cookies and prevents warm moisture condensing and making the cookies soggy. Traybakes are usually best left to cool in the tray before cutting into pieces and removing – although placing the baking tray on a wire rack will help to speed up the cooling process.

Most cookies are best eaten straight from the oven, but they also store well. As soon as the cookies are cool, pack then into an airtight container. This will help to keep soft cookies moist and dry cookies crisp. Unfilled and undecorated cookies can also be frozen. Freeze them in a single layer on baking trays, then transfer them to an airtight container and freeze until required. To thaw, transfer to a wire rack and leave at room temperature for 30 minutes.

classic cookies

These are the cookies and bars that have been
sampled and loved for decades – from peanut
butter cookies to tollhouse bars, biscotti to the
legendary neiman marcus chocolate chip cookie.
These are the simple essentials to any cookie-
maker's repertoire.

scottish shortbread

see variations page 41

Buttery, crumbly and simple to make – you'll love this version of classic shortbread. You can use the recipe to make cookies or as a base for cheesecakes or other desserts.

200 g (7 oz) plain flour
2 tbsp rice flour
175 g (6 oz) unsalted butter

100 g (3½ oz) caster sugar
2 tsp vanilla essence
2 tsp granulated sugar

Pre-heat the oven to 150°C (300°F / Gas mark 2). Line a 18 x 28-cm (7 x 11-in) tin with foil. Sift the plain flour into a large bowl and add the rice flour.

Beat the butter and the caster sugar until smooth. Add the vanilla essence and stir in the granulated sugar. Work the dough until it starts to clump together, then press it into the tin.

Bake for 45 to 50 minutes. The shortbread will look cooked before it actually is, so ensure that it bakes for the full 45 minutes.

Remove from the oven, sprinkle with granulated sugar and cut into fingers. Cool for 20 minutes and remove from the tin.

Store in an airtight container for up to five days.

Makes 1½ dozen

almond biscotti

see variations page 42

This twice-baked Italian biscuit can be enjoyed with coffee or served with sorbet as a dessert.

300 g (10 oz) plain flour
200 g (7 oz) caster sugar
1 tsp baking powder
¼ tsp salt

3 eggs
2 tsp vanilla essence
100 g (3½ oz) whole blanched almonds

Pre-heat the oven to 150°C (300°F / Gas mark 2). Grease and flour two baking sheets. Mix the dry ingredients together in a large bowl. Whisk the eggs and vanilla essence together then stir into the dry ingredients. Add the almonds and stir them into the dough. The dough should be sticky.

Divide the dough between the baking sheets and shape into two flat loaves about 25 cm (10 in) long and 5 cm (2 in) wide. Bake for 35 to 40 minutes until pale golden. Remove from the oven onto a chopping board and immediately slice into thin pieces about 1 cm (½ in) wide. Lay the slices back onto the baking sheets and cook for 10 to 15 minutes. Turn over each slice and cook for a further 10 to 15 minutes, or until the slices are golden brown. Remove from the oven and allow to cool.

When cool, store in an airtight container. The biscotti will keep for a couple of weeks.

Makes 3½ dozen

peanut butter cookies

see variations page 43

Rich and creamy, these cookies are a real indulgence for peanut butter fans.

200 g (7 oz) plain flour
½ tsp bicarbonate of soda
115 g (4 oz) unsalted butter
100 g (3½ oz) caster sugar

100 g (3½ oz) unrefined light brown sugar
1 egg
225 g (8 oz) crunchy peanut butter
Pinch of salt

Sift the flour and bicarbonate of soda together. In a separate bowl, beat the butter and sugars until soft and creamy. Combine the egg, flour mixture, peanut butter and salt. Add the butter and sugar mixture, and mix until smooth.

Wrap the dough in foil or parchment and refrigerate for at least two hours, preferably overnight.

Pre-heat the oven to 160°C (325°F / Gas mark 3).

Shape the dough into 3-cm (1¼-in) balls and place them 5 cm (2 in) apart on baking sheets. Flatten slightly with a fork. Bake for 15 minutes, or until golden.

Remove from the oven and allow to cool. Store in an airtight container for up to five days.

Makes 2 dozen

ginger nuts

see variations page 44

Crunchy and spicy, these sugar-crusted cookies are a sophisticated cookie treat.

50 g (2 oz) unsalted butter, melted and cooled
2 tbsp treacle
100 g (3½ oz) unrefined dark brown sugar
1 egg
150 g (5 oz) plain flour

1 tsp bicarbonate of soda
1 tsp ground ginger
¼ tsp ground allspice
Granulated sugar, to decorate

Pre-heat the oven to 175°C (350°F / Gas mark 4). Mix the cooled melted butter, treacle, unrefined dark brown sugar and egg in a large bowl. Sift the remaining dry ingredients together and stir into the butter mixture.

Using about 1½ tablespoons of dough at a time, form the dough into balls. Place the balls 5 cm (2 in) apart on a non-stick baking sheet or use parchment on a standard baking sheet. Lightly press the cookies into 3-cm (1¼-in) rounds.

Refrigerate the cookies for one hour before baking. Sprinkle with granulated sugar and bake for 10 to 12 minutes. The cookies will puff up, then settle when cooked. Transfer the cookies to a wire rack to cool. Store in an airtight container for up to five days.

Makes 1½ dozen

linzer cookies

see variations page 45

These cookies originated from the sweet pastry used to make Austria's Linzer tart.

150 g (5 oz) roasted skinned hazelnuts
300 g (10 oz) plain flour
100 g (3½ oz) granulated sugar
¼ tsp salt
2 tsp ground cinnamon

¼ tsp ground cloves
225 g (8 oz) unsalted butter
Grated zest of 1 lemon (2 to 3 tsp)
50 g (2 oz) raspberry jam
2 tbsp icing sugar

Pre-heat the oven to 175°C (350°F / Gas mark 4). Grind the hazelnuts in a food processor until fine. Add the flour, granulated sugar, salt, cinnamon, cloves and butter to the food processor and pulse until the mixture looks crumbly. Add the lemon, and blend until the mixture clumps together.

Work the dough into a flat round, shape, wrap in parchment and refrigerate for 30 minutes, or until firm. On a floured surface, roll out the dough to 3 mm (⅛ in) thick. Using a cookie cutter, cut out shapes, ensuring you have equal numbers of each shape. Place half the cookies on parchment-lined baking sheets and cut out a hole in each centre. Bake the cookies with the cut-out centres separately from the remaining cookies for 8 to 10 minutes. Sandwich the cooled cookies together with raspberry jam. Using a small piping bag, fill with jam and top up the cut-out centres with jam. Decorate the cookies with the icing sugar. Store filled cookies for up to two days and unfilled cookies for up to a week.

Makes 1½ dozen

snicker doodles

see variations page 46

Snicker doodles are delicate cookies – but pile your plate high, as one is never enough.

190 g (6½ oz) plain flour
1 tsp cream of tartar
½ tsp bicarbonate of soda
1 tsp ground cinnamon

¼ tsp salt
225 g (8 oz) unsalted butter
165 g (5½ oz) caster sugar
1 egg

Pre-heat the oven to 200°C (400°F / Gas mark 6). Sift the flour, cream of tartar, bicarbonate of soda and half the cinnamon together in a bowl, then add the salt. In a separate bowl, beat the butter and all but 2 tablespoons of the sugar. Add the egg.

Combine the dry ingredients with the butter mixture and mix to a smooth paste. Wrap the dough in parchment and refrigerate for about 30 minutes, or until firm. Mix together the remaining sugar and the cinnamon. Shape the dough into small balls and roll in the cinnamon sugar.

Place the balls at least 5 cm (2 in) apart, as the mixture spreads to produce a thin cookie. Flatten each cookie slightly with a fork. Bake for 10 to 12 minutes. Cool for five minutes.

Store in an airtight container for up to five days.

Makes 2 dozen

beacon hill cookies

see variations page 47

Chocolate lover? Try these light and sticky ultra-chocolately cookies.

150 g (5 oz) dark chocolate
2 egg whites
⅛ tsp cream of tartar

50 g (2 oz) caster sugar
100 g (3½ oz) chopped pecans
½ tsp vanilla essence

Pre-heat the oven to 175°C (350°F / Gas mark 4).

Melt the chocolate. Beat the egg whites with the cream of tartar until soft peaks form. Add one third of the sugar, beat for a further minute, then add one third more of the sugar. Beat until the whites are stiff and fold in the remaining sugar.

Fold the nuts, chocolate and vanilla into the mixture.

Drop level teaspoonfuls of the mixture onto parchment-lined baking sheets 4 cm (1½ in) apart. Bake for 10 to 12 minutes until the cookies are cracked and firm to touch. Lift the parchment sheets onto wire racks and allow the cookies to cool.

Store in an airtight container for up to three days.

Makes 2½ dozen

neiman marcus cookies

see variations page 48

The rumour that gave this cookie its rise to fame tells of a customer who inadvertently paid $250 US for this cookie recipe, thinking she was being charged $2.50 US.

115 g (4 oz) unsalted butter
200 g (7 oz) light brown sugar
1 egg
2 tsp vanilla essence
200 g (7 oz) plain flour

½ tsp bicarbonate of soda
½ tsp baking powder
¼ tsp salt
1½ tsp instant coffee powder
225 g (8 oz) plain chocolate chips

Pre-heat the oven to 190°C (375°F / Gas mark 5).

Beat the butter and sugar together, and add the egg and vanilla essence.

Sift together the remaining dry ingredients, including the coffee powder. Stir the dry ingredients into the butter mixture and mix in the chocolate chips.

Roll into balls. Use your fingers to flatten onto a non-stick baking sheet 5 cm (2 in) apart. Bake for 8 to 10 minutes. Cool for five minutes.

Store in an airtight container for four to five days.

Makes 2 dozen

butter cookies

see variations page 49

Simple, rich and buttery – use only the best quality ingredients for these cookies.

225 g (8 oz) unsalted butter
150 g (5 oz) caster sugar
1½ tsp vanilla essence
¼ tsp salt
300 g (10 oz) plain flour

Pre-heat the oven to 175°C (350°F / Gas mark 4).

Beat the butter, sugar and vanilla until smooth and creamy, but not fluffy.

Add the salt and flour and mix to a smooth paste.

Shape the dough into a log about 4 cm (1½ in) thick, wrap in foil and refrigerate for two hours until the dough is firm. When ready to bake the cookies, cut the log into 6-mm (¼-in) thick slices. Place the slices 4 cm (1½ in) apart on a non-stick baking sheet or use parchment on a standard baking sheet. Bake for 12 to 14 minutes.

Cool on a wire rack and store in an airtight container for up to five days.

Makes 2½ dozen

anzac biscuits

see variations page 50

Originally baked annually on April 25th in Australia to commemorate the fallen soldiers at Gallipoli in 1915–1916 during World War I, these cookies are now popular worldwide.

100 g (3½ oz) rolled oats
150 g (5 oz) plain flour
100 g (3½ oz) unrefined light brown sugar
50 g (2 oz) flaked coconut

115 g (4 oz) unsalted butter
2 tbsp golden syrup
½ tsp bicarbonate of soda
1 tbsp hot water

Pre-heat the oven to 175°C (350°F / Gas mark 4). Line two baking sheets with parchment.

Mix the oats, flour, sugar and coconut together in a bowl.

Melt the butter and golden syrup in a saucepan over a low heat. Mix the bicarbonate of soda with the hot water and stir into the butter mixture. Pour the hot butter mixture into the dry ingredients.

Drop tablespoons of the dough onto the sheets 5 cm (2 in) apart and flatten slightly with a fork. Bake for 10 to 12 minutes until golden. Cool for five minutes.

Store in an airtight container for up to five days.

Makes 1½ dozen

tollhouse cookies

see variations page 51

These legendary bars are based on the first American chocolate chip cookie recipe.

340 g (11½ oz) plain flour
1 tsp bicarbonate of soda
½ tsp salt
225 g (8 oz) unsalted butter
150 g (5 oz) granulated sugar

150 g (5 oz) unrefined light brown sugar
2 tsp vanilla essence
2 eggs
200 g (7 oz) chopped pecans
150 g (5 oz) dark chocolate chips

Pre-heat the oven to 190°C (375°F / Gas mark 5). Grease and line a 23 x 33-cm (9 x 13-in) tin.

Sift together the flour, bicarbonate of soda and salt.

Beat the butter and sugars together with the vanilla essence. Beat in the eggs. Stir the flour mixture, nuts and chocolate chips into the mixture.

Spoon the mixture into the tin. Bake for 25 minutes until golden and firm. Cool in the tin for five minutes and cut into squares. Remove from the tin and cool on a wire rack.

Store in an airtight container for three to four days.

Makes 1 dozen

pretzels

see variations page 52

These are great fun to make and easy to modify – try dividing up the dough and making different flavoured pretzels.

300 g (10 oz) plain flour
2 tbsp caster sugar
2 tsp active dried yeast
240 ml (8½ fl oz) warm water

150 g (2 oz) unsalted butter, melted and cooled
½ tsp salt
1 egg yolk
2 tbsp granulated sugar

Pre-heat the oven to 190°C (375°F / Gas mark 5). Mix 4 tablespoons of the flour with the caster sugar and dried yeast. Add the warm water and mix to a paste. Put in a warm place for five minutes.

Add the yeast mixture and butter to the remaining flour and salt, and mix well. Knead on a floured surface for five minutes. Allow the dough to rise in a greased bowl in a warm place for 30 minutes. Divide the dough into 24 pieces. Roll and form each piece into a pretzel shape. Place on a greased baking sheet, mix the egg yolk with 1 tablespoon water and brush the mixture onto the pretzels. Sprinkle with granulated sugar and bake for 10 minutes or until golden.

Cool on wire racks and store in an airtight container for two to three days.

Makes 2 dozen

rocky road

see variations page 53

Simple to bake, everyone will love this sweet and sticky snack.

75 g (3 oz) unsalted butter
150 g (5 oz) crumbled digestive biscuits
2 tbsp caster sugar

100 g (3½ oz) chopped pecans
200 g (7 oz) miniature marshmallows
150 g (5 oz) plain chocolate chips

Pre-heat the oven to 175°C (350°F / Gas mark 4).

Melt the butter and add the digestive biscuit crumbs and sugar. Press into the base of a 20-cm (8-in) square tin lined with foil.

Sprinkle the pecans over the crust and bake for 10 minutes. Leaving the oven on, remove the bars from the oven and scatter the marshmallows and chocolate chips over the crust.

Return the tin to the oven for about 10 minutes until the marshmallow melts. Cool completely before removing from the tin and cutting into squares.

Store in an airtight container for three to four days.

Makes 1½ dozen

scottish shortbread

see base recipe page 19

orange shortbread
Prepare the basic shortbread dough, but reduce the vanilla essence
to 1 teaspoon and add the zest of 1 orange (2 to 3 teaspoons).

cinnamon shortbread
Prepare the basic shortbread dough, but reduce the vanilla essence
to 1 teaspoon and add 1 teaspoon ground cinnamon.

hazelnut shortbread
Prepare the basic shortbread dough, reducing the plain flour to
190 g (6½ oz) and adding 50 g (2 oz) toasted finely ground hazelnuts.

chocolate-dipped shortbread fingers
Prepare the basic shortbread dough and bake, but omit sprinkling the
sugar after baking. Cut the shortbread into fingers and half-dip each
finger into melted dark chocolate. Remove any excess chocolate from
the base of each piece and place the shortbread fingers onto parchment
until the chocolate sets. Store as for ordinary shortbread.

variations

almond biscotti

see base recipe page 20

lemon & pistachio biscotti
Prepare the basic biscotti dough, substituting the grated zest of 1 lemon
(2 to 3 teaspoons) for the vanilla essence and pistachios for the almonds.

chocolate chip & raisin biscotti
Prepare the basic biscotti dough, substituting 75 g (3 oz) raisins and
75 g (3 oz) plain chocolate chips for the almonds.

fig & fennel biscotti
Prepare the basic biscotti dough, substituting 75 g (3 oz) chopped dried figs
for half the almonds and 2 teaspoons fennel seeds for the vanilla essence.

variations

peanut butter cookies

see base recipe page 23

peanut butter & chocolate chip cookies
Prepare the basic cookie dough and add 75 g (3 oz) dark chocolate chips.

cream cheese topped peanut butter cookies
Prepare and bake the basic cookie dough. When cool, mix 200 g (7 oz) cream cheese with 2 tablespoons icing sugar and spread the cookies with the cream cheese topping. Sprinkle with a few plain chocolate chips. The cookies are best eaten the same day. If not, refrigerate and eat the next day.

variations

ginger nuts

see base recipe page 24

light ginger nuts
Prepare the basic cookie dough, substituting golden syrup for the treacle.
Add 2 tablespoons chopped crystallised ginger.

ginger & walnut cookies
Prepare the basic cookie dough and add 50 g (2 oz) chopped walnuts.

pineapple & ginger cookies
Prepare the basic cookie dough and add 75 g (3 oz) chopped crystallised
pineapple.

ginger, rum & coconut cookies
Prepare the basic cookie dough and add 2 tablespoons dark rum and
substitute 25 g (1 oz) flaked coconut for 40 g (1½ oz) plain flour.

variations

linzer cookies

see base recipe page 27

lemon linzer cookies
Prepare the basic cookie dough, double the grated lemon zest
(4 to 6 teaspoons) and when baked, fill the cookies with lemon curd.
Dust with icing sugar.

apple linzer cookies
Prepare the basic cookie recipe and when baked, sandwich the cookies
together with apple fruit spread instead of raspberry jam. Dust with
icing sugar.

almond linzer cookies
Prepare the basic cookie dough, substituting almonds for the hazelnuts.
Use raspberry jam to fill the cookies and then dust with icing sugar.

variations

snicker doodles

see base recipe page 28

raisin snicker doodles
Prepare the basic cookie dough and add 75 g (3 oz) raisins.

chocolate & vanilla snicker doodles
Prepare the basic cookie dough and add 2 teaspoons vanilla essence
and 75 g (3 oz) dark chocolate chips.

ginger snicker doodles
Prepare the basic cookie dough and add 3 tablespoons chopped
crystallised ginger.

beacon hill cookies

see base recipe page 31

spiced beacon hill cookies
Prepare the basic cookie dough and add 1 teaspoon ground cinnamon.

double chocolate beacon hill cookies
Prepare the basic cookie dough and add 75 g (3 oz) white chocolate chips.

cherry & walnut beacon hill cookies
Prepare the basic cookie dough and add 75 g (3 oz) dried cherries. Substitute walnuts for the pecans.

variations

neiman marcus cookies

see base recipe page 32

neiman marcus crunch cookies
Prepare the basic cookie dough and add 50 g (2 oz) crushed hard
toffee bars.

neiman marcus berry cookies
Prepare the basic cookie dough, omitting the coffee and add 75 g (3 oz)
dried blueberries and 75 g (3 oz) dried cranberries.

neiman marcus ultra chocolate cookies
Prepare the basic cookie dough, substituting Dutch process cocoa powder
for the coffee and adding 75 g (3 oz) dark chocolate chips and 75 g (3 oz)
white chocolate chips.

variations

butter cookies

see base recipe page 34

butter almond cookies
Prepare the basic cookie dough and substitute almond essence for the
vanilla essence.

lemon & cinnamon butter cookies
Prepare the basic cookie dough, but reduce the vanilla essence by half
and add the grated zest of 1 lemon (2 to 3 teaspoons) and 1 teaspoon
ground cinnamon.

ginger butter cookies
Prepare the basic cookie dough, but reduce the vanilla essence by half
and add 1 teaspoon ground ginger to the flour, then 3 tablespoons chopped
crystallised ginger after the flour is added.

anzac biscuits

see base recipe page 35

macadamia anzac biscuits
Prepare the basic cookie dough, but reduce the flaked coconut by half and add 40 g (1½ oz) chopped macadamia nuts.

cherry anzac biscuits
Prepare the basic cookie dough and add 150 g (2 oz) chopped red glacé cherries.

chocolate chip anzac biscuits
Prepare the basic cookie dough and add 75 g (3 oz) plain chocolate chips.

variations

tollhouse cookies

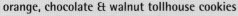

see base recipe page 37

orange, chocolate & walnut tollhouse cookies
Prepare the basic cookie dough and add the grated zest of 1 orange
(2 to 3 teaspoons). Substitute 3 tablespoons cocoa powder for an equal
quantity of flour and walnuts for the pecans.

white chocolate & hazelnut tollhouse cookies
Prepare the basic cookie dough, but substitute hazelnuts for the pecans and
white chocolate chips for the dark chocolate chips.

mocha tollhouse cookies
Prepare the basic cookie dough, substituting 3 tablespoons cocoa powder for
an equal quantity of flour and add 1 tablespoon instant powdered coffee.

variations

pretzels

see base recipe page 38

caraway & orange pretzels
Prepare the basic pretzel dough and after allowing it to rise add 2 teaspoons caraway seeds and 2 tablespoons chopped crystallised orange.

chocolate chip pretzels
Prepare the basic pretzel dough and after allowing it to rise add 75 g (3 oz) dark chocolate chips.

spiced pretzels
Prepare the basic pretzel dough and add 1 teaspoon ground allspice and 1 teaspoon ground ginger.

variations

rocky road

see base recipe page 40

cherry rocky road
Prepare the basic cookie dough and add 150 g (5 oz) red glacé cherries
before adding the marshmallows.

pink rocky road
Prepare the basic cookie dough, but substitute white chocolate chips
for the plain chocolate chips, add 75 g (3 oz) dried cherries and add
pink marshmallows.

caramel fudge rocky road
Prepare and bake the crust. Drizzle the crust with 4 tablespoons caramel
sauce and 75 g (3 oz) chopped fudge pieces before topping with chocolate
chips and marshmallows.

peanut rocky road
Prepare the crust and substitute chopped peanuts for the pecans. When
the crust is baked, spoon 125 g (4½ oz) peanut butter over the crust before
topping with chocolate chips and marshmallows.

teatime cookies

Cookies were made for eating at teatime, whether with a glass of milk or a mid-afternoon cup of tea. This chapter is full of traditional teatime cookies, from lemon fingers to Viennese pockets, ginger crumble cookies to hazelnut chewies.

ginger crumble cookies

see variations page 78

Crisp on the outside and chewy in the middle, these little cookies are packed with spice.

for the cookies

50 g (2 oz) unsalted butter, melted
2 tbsp treacle
100 g (3½ oz) dark brown sugar
1 egg
150 g (5 oz) plain flour
1 tsp bicarbonate of soda
1 tsp ground ginger
½ tsp ground cinnamon

¼ tsp ground allspice
2 tbsp finely chopped crystallised ginger

for the crumble topping

40 g (1½ oz) unsalted butter
5 tbsp plain flour
3 tbsp rolled oats
3 tbsp light brown sugar

Pre-heat the oven to 175°C (350°F / Gas mark 4). Mix the cooled melted butter, treacle, sugar and egg in a large bowl. Sift the remaining dry ingredients together and stir into the butter mixture. Add the crystallised ginger. In a separate bowl, combine all the ingredients for the topping.

Roll the cookie dough into balls, using 1½ tablespoons of dough at a time. Place the balls 5 cm (2 in) apart on a non-stick baking sheet. Lightly press the cookies into 3-cm (1¼-in) rounds and press 1 to 2 teaspoons of the topping onto the dough. Refrigerate the cookies for one hour before baking. Bake for 10 to 12 minutes – the cookies will puff up, then settle down when baked. Cool on a wire rack. Store in an airtight container for three to four days.

Makes 1½ dozen

lemon finger cookies

see variations page 79

Serve these elegant, pale lemon fingers with a scented cup of Earl Grey tea.

for the cookies

225 g (8 oz) unsalted butter
50 g (2 oz) icing sugar
½ tsp vanilla essence
Grated zest of 3 lemons (6 to 9 tsp)
225 g (8 oz) plain flour
3 tbsp cornflour

for the filling

50 g (2 oz) unsalted butter
125 g (4½ oz) icing sugar
Grated zest of 2 lemons (4 to 6 tsp)
Juice of ½ lemon (2 tbsp)

Pre-heat the oven to 175°C (350°F / Gas mark 4). Beat the butter, icing sugar, vanilla essence and lemon zest together until light and fluffy. Sift the flour and cornflour together and stir into the creamed mixture. Using a 1-cm (½-in) fluted nozzle and piping bag, pipe the mixture into 5-cm (2-in) fingers arranged 4 cm (1½ in) apart on a non-stick baking sheet. Bake the cookies for 12 minutes. Allow them to firm up before transferring them to a wire rack to cool.

To make the filling, beat the butter and icing sugar with the lemon zest and juice until light and fluffy. Spread the filling onto the flat side of one cookie, then put another cookie on top, flat side down, and sandwich together.

Store unfilled for four to five days, filled for two to three days.

Makes 8 filled cookies

turnover cookies

see variations page 80

Delicate half-moon pastry on the outside, rich and indulgent filling on the inside.

for the cookies

200 g (7 oz) plain flour
100 g (3½ oz) self-raising flour, sifted
50 g (2 oz) white vegetable fat
175 g (6 oz) unsalted butter, diced
50 g (2 oz) caster sugar
2 egg yolks

for the filling

350 g (12 oz) cream cheese
1½ tsp ground cinnamon
150 g (5 oz) raisins
1 egg white
4 tbsp granulated sugar

Pre-heat the oven to 190°C (375°F / Gas mark 5). Grease two baking sheets. Sift the flours and rub in the fats until the mixture resembles fine breadcrumbs. Add half the sugar. Mix in the egg yolks and 1 to 2 tablespoons of water. Mix to a smooth dough. Wrap in parchment and refrigerate for 20 minutes.

Mix the cream cheese with the remaining sugar, cinnamon and raisins. Roll out the pastry to 6 mm (¼ in) thick and cut out rounds using a 5-cm (2-in) cutter. Fill each pastry round with a small amount of filling. Dampen the edges with water and fold in half to give a half-moon shape. Brush with egg white, sprinkle with granulated sugar and bake for 10 to 12 minutes.

Cool on a wire rack. Best eaten fresh. Store leftovers in the refrigerator for one to two days.

Makes 2 dozen

jam drops

see variations page 81

These jam drops are simple to make and perfect with a cup of herbal tea and a good book before bed.

115 g (4 oz) unsalted butter
150 g (5 oz) caster sugar
1 egg

200 g (7 oz) plain flour
½ tsp baking powder
75 g (3 oz) jam, any flavour

Pre-heat the oven to 175°C (350°F / Gas mark 4). Line two baking sheets with parchment.

Beat the butter and sugar until light and fluffy. Add the egg and beat well.

Sift the flour and baking powder and stir into the butter mixture. Roll the mixture into balls and place them at least 5 cm (2 in) apart on the baking sheets.

Press a finger into each ball and fill the hole with a little jam. Bake for 10 minutes until golden. Add a little more jam while the cookies are still warm.

Cool on a wire rack. Store in an airtight container for four to five days.

Makes 2 dozen

viennese pockets

see variations page 82

For a luxurious dessert, drizzle with royal icing and accompany with coffee.

for the filling

4 tbsp milk
150 g (5 oz) caster sugar
115 g (4 oz) ground toasted hazelnuts
25 g (1 oz) unsalted butter
2 tbsp dark rum

for the cookies

375 g (13 oz) plain flour
200 g (7 oz) unsalted butter
Grated zest of 1 lemon (2 to 3 tsp)
1 egg
1 egg white
2 tbsp granulated sugar

Line two baking sheets with parchment. Heat the milk in a saucepan with 50 g (2 oz) of the caster sugar. Stir until the sugar is dissolved and bring to the boil. Remove from the heat and stir in the hazelnuts, butter and half the rum. Leave the nut filling to cool, then refrigerate until firm. Preheat the oven to 175°C (350°F / Gas mark 4).

Sift the flour into a bowl, combine with the remaining caster sugar and rub in the butter. Add the lemon zest and the remaining rum and egg. Mix the dough to a paste. Wrap in parchment and chill the dough for 30 minutes. Roll out the dough to 3 mm (⅛ in) thick and cut into 5-cm (2-in) squares. Place 2 teaspoons of cooled nut mixture into the centre of each square. Fold each corner into the centre and press to seal. Brush the squares with egg white and sprinkle with granulated sugar. Bake for 20 minutes. Remove from the oven onto wire racks. When cool, store in an airtight container for five days.

Makes 2 dozen

hazelnut chewies

see variations page 83

These small nutty cookies will add a warm and flavourful taste to your afternoon tea.

150 g (5 oz) ground toasted hazelnuts
125 g (4¼ oz) icing sugar

4 egg whites
¼ tsp cream of tartar

Pre-heat the oven to 190°C (375°F / Gas mark 5). Line two baking sheets with parchment.

Put the hazelnuts and sugar in a saucepan.

Beat the egg whites with the cream of tartar until stiff and combine with the hazelnuts in the saucepan. Place the pan over a moderate heat and cook for 5 to 10 minutes until the mixture starts to come away from the sides of the pan.

Spoon the mixture into rough mounds on the parchment 5 cm (2 in) apart. Bake for 10 minutes. Transfer to a wire rack and cool for 10 minutes.

Store in an airtight container for five to six days.

Makes 2 dozen

polenta crescents

see variations page 84

With a hint of lemon, polenta cookies offer a refreshing change from the often sugary teatime snacks.

115 g (4 oz) unsalted butter
100 g (3½ oz) icing sugar
2 egg yolks
Grated zest of 1 lemon (2 to 3 tsp)

2 tsp vanilla essence
150 g (5 oz) plain flour
Pinch of baking powder
50 g (2 oz) finely ground polenta

Pre-heat the oven to 160°C (325°F / Gas mark 3). Grease two baking sheets. Beat the butter and sugar together until light and fluffy. Add egg yolks, lemon zest and vanilla essence.

In a separate bowl, sift the flour and baking powder together and mix in the polenta. Add to the butter mixture and mix to a smooth dough.

Roll the dough into 1-cm- (½-in-) thick lengths and cut into 10-cm (4-in) pieces. Shape these into crescents and space them 5 cm (2 in) apart on the baking sheets. Bake for 15 minutes until pale in colour. Cool on wire racks.

Store in an airtight container for five to seven days.

Makes 2 dozen

butter sandwich cookies

see variations page 85

Delectable butter cookies with a light creamy filling.

for the cookies

300 g (10 oz) unsalted butter
150 g (5 oz) caster sugar
1½ tsp vanilla essence
1 egg
¼ tsp salt
300 g (10 oz) plain flour

for the filling

75 g (3 oz) icing sugar
3 tbsp cream cheese
4 tbsp raspberry jam
Extra icing sugar, to decorate

Preheat the oven to 175°C (350°F / Gas mark 4). Beat all but 25 g (1 oz) of the butter with the sugar and vanilla until creamy but not fluffy. Beat in the egg. Add salt and flour and mix to a smooth paste. Shape the dough into a flat round, wrap and refrigerate for 30 minutes.

Roll out the dough on a lightly floured surface 3-mm (⅛-in) thick and cut out 5-cm (2-in) rounds. Place the rounds 2.5 cm (1 in) apart on a non-stick baking sheet. Bake for 12 to 15 minutes. Cool on a wire rack.

Beat the remaining butter and sifted icing sugar until the mixture is pale and soft. Stir in the cream cheese. Spread half of the cookies with the jam and half with the cream cheese mixture. Sandwich and serve dusted with icing sugar. Store in an airtight container for five to seven days.

Makes 1½ dozen

white chocolate & orange cookies

see variations page 86

Delicate chocolate and aromatic orange makes this an elegant accompaniment to a late afternoon cup of tea.

115 g (4 oz) unsalted butter
200 g (7 oz) caster sugar
1 egg
Grated zest of 1 orange (2 to 3 tsp)
1 tsp vanilla essence

200 g (7 oz) plain flour
½ tsp bicarbonate of soda
¼ tsp baking powder
¼ tsp salt
225 g (8 oz) white chocolate chips/dark

Pre-heat the oven to 190°C (375°F / Gas mark 5). Beat the butter and sugar. Add the egg, orange zest and vanilla essence.

Sift together the dry ingredients. Stir the dry ingredients and chocolate chips into the butter mixture and combine.

Roll into balls. Use your fingers to flatten onto a non-stick baking sheet 5 cm (2 in) apart. Bake for 8 to 10 minutes. Cool for five minutes.

When cool, store in an airtight container for up to four to five days.

Makes 2 dozen

pine nut bites

see variations page 87

Bite-sized with added pine nut crunch, these cookies are the perfect antidote for a mid-afternoon snack craving.

300 g (10 oz) ground almonds
300 g (10 oz) caster sugar
3 egg whites
200 g (7 oz) pine nuts

Pre-heat the oven to 200°C (400°F / Gas mark 6).

Mix together the almonds, sugar and two of the egg whites until the dough is smooth and pliable.

Roll the almond dough into small balls, dip them in the remaining egg white and then into the pine nuts.

Put the balls onto a parchment-lined baking sheet 4 cm (1½ in) apart. Bake for 5 to 10 minutes until golden and firm. Transfer to a wire rack and cool.

Store in an airtight container for four to five days.

Makes 2 dozen

melting moments

see variations page 88

The double filling in these small cookies makes for twice the flavour!

for the cookies

225 g (8 oz) softened unsalted butter
50 g (2 oz) icing sugar
½ tsp vanilla essence
225 g (8 oz) plain flour
3 tbsp cornflour

for the filling

50 g (2 oz) unsalted butter
125 g (4½ oz) icing sugar
2 tsp vanilla essence
3 tbsp fruit jam, any flavour

Pre-heat the oven to 175°C (350°F / Gas mark 4). Beat the butter, icing sugar and vanilla essence together until light and fluffy. Sift the flour and cornflour and stir into the creamed mixture. Using a 1-cm (⅓-in) fluted nozzle and piping bag, pipe the mixture into 2½-cm (1-in) rosettes 4 cm (1½ in) apart on a non-stick baking sheet.

Bake for 10 to 12 minutes until golden. Allow the cookies to firm up slightly before transferring them to a wire rack to cool.

Beat the butter and icing sugar together with the vanilla essence until light and fluffy. Spread fruit jam onto the bottom of half the cookies and then spread or pipe the filling onto the other halves. Sandwich together. Store in an airtight container for three to four days.

Makes 1½ dozen

jam coconut squares

see variations page 89

This coconut and jam combination makes these treats especially moist and chewy.

115 g (4 oz) unsalted butter
100 g (3½ oz) caster sugar
150 g (5 oz) plain flour, sifted
½ tsp baking powder
1 egg yolk

125 g (4½ oz) jam
2 eggs
1 tbsp cornflour
100 g (3½ oz) flaked coconut
200 ml (7 fl oz) coconut cream

Pre-heat the oven to 175°C (350°F / Gas mark 4). Combine the butter, half of the sugar, flour and baking powder in a food processor for one to two minutes. Add the egg yolk.

Process until the mixture forms a smooth dough. Cut a piece of parchment to line a 20 x 30-cm (8 x 10-in) tin. Roll out the dough on the parchment and then lift into the tin. Prick with a fork before refrigerating for 10 minutes to set. Bake 12 to 15 minutes until golden. Remove from the oven, but keep the oven on.

Spread with your favourite jam. Beat the remaining sugar, eggs and cornflour together. Add the flaked coconut and coconut cream and pour over the jam. Bake for another 15 minutes until firm to touch. To finish, grill on a high heat for three to four minutes until golden.

When cool, cut into squares. Store in an airtight container for three to four days.

Makes 2 dozen

variations

ginger crumble cookies

see base recipe page 55

ginger walnut crumble cookies
Prepare the basic cookie dough and add 100 g (3½ oz) chopped walnuts.

maple ginger cookies
Prepare the basic cookie dough, substituting maple syrup for the treacle.
Serve without the crumble topping.

maple apple crumble cookies
Prepare the basic cookie dough, substituting maple syrup for the treacle.
Increase the cinnamon to 1½ teaspoons and replace the crystallised ginger
with 50 g (2 oz) chopped dried apple pieces.

lemon finger cookies

see base recipe page 56

lemon & chocolate finger cookies
Prepare the basic cookie recipe and assemble the filled cookies in the same way. Half-dip the fingers (on a diagonal) into melted dark chocolate. Place on parchment until the chocolate sets.

spiced lemon finger cookies
Prepare the basic cookie dough, adding ½ teaspoon ground cinnamon to the flour.

lemon & cream cheese filled cookie fingers
Prepare the basic cookie dough. For the filling, beat 200 g (7 oz) cream cheese and 1 tablespoon icing sugar together and stir in the grated zest of 1 lemon (2 to 3 teaspoons) and 3 tablespoons lemon curd. Sandwich the cookie fingers with the filling.

variations

turnover cookies

see base recipe page 59

cream cheese & jam turnovers
Prepare the basic cookie dough, omitting the raisins from the cream cheese filling. When filling the turnovers, add ½ teaspoon fruit jam to the cream cheese.

apple turnovers
Prepare the basic cookie dough, adding 1 teaspoon ground cinnamon and the grated zest of 1 lemon (2 to 3 teaspoons) to the flour. Mix 75 g (3 oz) apple butter and raisins and fill the turnovers.

blueberry turnovers
Prepare the basic cookie dough and substitute blueberries for the raisins.

lemon curd turnovers
Prepare the basic cookie recipe and fill the turnovers with lemon curd instead of cream cheese.

variations

jam drops

see base recipe page 60

lemon curd drops
Prepare the basic cookie dough and substitute lemon curd for the jam.

apple & cinnamon drops
Prepare the basic cookie dough and add ½ teaspoon ground cinnamon to the flour. Fill the drops with apple butter or fruit spread instead of jam.

chocolate drops
Prepare the basic cookie dough, substituting 2 tablespoons Dutch process cocoa powder for an equal quantity of the flour. Fill each drop with chocolate-hazelnut spread instead of jam.

raisin jam drops
Prepare the basic cookie dough, adding 75 g (3 oz) raisins to the dough.

variations

viennese pockets

see base recipe page 63

viennese pockets with pecans & chocolate chips
Prepare the basic cookie recipe, substituting pecans for the hazelnuts, and adding 75 g (3 oz) dark chocolate chips to the filling.

viennese pockets with cream cheese & poppy seeds
Prepare the basic cookie recipe. For the filling, mix 115 g (4 oz) cream cheese with 1 tablespoon poppy seeds and 2 tablespoons breadcrumbs. Use to fill the squares.

viennese pockets with apple
Prepare the basic cookie recipe. For the filling, peel and finely chop two apples and mix with 1 teaspoon ground cinnamon and 2 tablespoons raisins. Use to fill the squares.

viennese pockets with chocolate & cherries
Prepare the basic cookie recipe, substituting 50 g (2 oz) chopped red glacé cherries for half the hazelnuts and adding 75 g (3 oz) dark chocolate chips to the filling.

hazelnut chewies

see base recipe page 64

hazelnut & apricot chewies
Prepare the basic cookie dough. Fold in 75 g (3 oz) chopped dried
apricots to the mixture before it is baked.

brazil nut & chocolate chip chewies
Prepare the basic cookie dough, substituting brazil nuts for the hazelnuts.
Fold in 75 g (3 oz) dark chocolate chips to the mixture before it is baked.

almond & cranberry chewies
Prepare the basic cookie dough, substituting almonds for the hazelnuts.
Fold in 75 g (3 oz) dried cranberries to the mixture before it is baked.

macadamia & pineapple chewies
Prepare the basic cookie dough, substituting macadamias for the
hazelnuts. Fold in 75 g (3 oz) chopped dried pineapple to the mixture before
it is baked.

variations

polenta crescents

see base recipe page 67

chocolate-dipped polenta crescents
When the baked cookies have cooled, half-dip them in melted dark chocolate. Remove the excess chocolate and lay them on parchment until the chocolate sets.

oatmeal crescents
Prepare the basic cookie dough, substituting oatmeal for the polenta and 1 teaspoon ground cinnamon for the lemon zest.

orange & chocolate chip crescents
Prepare the basic cookie dough, substituting orange zest for the lemon zest and adding 75 g (3 oz) dark chocolate chips.

nut crescents with chocolate-hazelnut filling
Prepare the basic cookie dough, substituting ground hazelnuts for the polenta. Bake and cool the cookies. Spread half the cookie bases with chocolate-hazelnut spread and sandwich together with the remaining halves.

variations

butter sandwich cookies

see base recipe page 68

orange butter cookies
Prepare the basic cookie dough and add the grated zest of 1 orange
(2 to 3 teaspoons). Prepare the filling and add the grated zest of 1 orange
(2 to 3 teaspoons). Fill and sandwich the cookies.

maple butter cookies with pecan filling
Prepare the basic cookie dough and substitute maple syrup for half of
the sugar. Prepare the filling and add 2 tablespoons bourbon whisky and
50 g (2 oz) chopped pecans. Fill and sandwich the cookies.

spiced butter cookies
Prepare the basic cookie dough and add 1 teaspoon ground cinnamon.
Prepare the filling and sandwich together.

variations

white chocolate & orange cookies

see base recipe page 71

white chocolate & peanut butter cookies
Prepare the basic cookie dough, omitting the orange zest and adding 50 g (2 oz) smooth peanut butter.

dark chocolate & orange cookies
Prepare the basic cookie dough and use dark chocolate chips instead of the white chocolate chips.

white chocolate, orange & cranberry cookies
Prepare the basic cookie dough, adding 75 g (3 oz) dried cranberries.

variations

pine nut bites

see base recipe page 72

lemon & pine nut bites
Prepare the basic cookie dough and add the grated zest of 1 lemon
(2 to 3 teaspoons).

chocolate chip pine nut bites
Prepare the basic cookie dough and add 75 g (3 oz) dark chocolate chips.

cherry & walnut bites
Prepare the basic cookie dough and add 50 g (2 oz) chopped red glacé
cherries to the almond mixture. Substitute chopped walnuts for the
pine nuts.

variations

melting moments

see base recipe page 75

malted milk melting moments
Prepare the basic cookie dough, substituting 2 tablespoons
malted milk powder for 2 tablespoons of the flour in the cookie
recipe, and 2 tablespoons malted milk powder for 2 tablespoons of
the icing sugar in the filling. Omit the fruit jam.

mocha melting moments
Prepare the basic cookie dough, substituting 2 teaspoons instant coffee
powder for the vanilla essence, and 2 tablespoons cooled melted dark
chocolate for the vanilla essence in the filling. Omit the fruit jam.

ginger melting moments
Prepare the basic cookie dough, substituting 1 teaspoon ground ginger
for the vanilla essence in the cookie recipe, and adding 2 tablespoons
chopped crystallised ginger to the filling. Omit the fruit jam.

variations

jam coconut squares

see base recipe page 76

coconut & chocolate squares
Prepare the basic cookie dough and substitute chocolate-hazelnut spread
for the jam. Add 75 g (3 oz) plain chocolate chips to the coconut topping.

pineapple & coconut squares
Prepare the basic cookie dough and use pineapple jam. Add 50 g (2 oz)
chopped crystallised pineapple to the coconut topping.

rum & coconut squares
Prepare the basic cookie dough and add 2 tablespoons dark rum to the
coconut topping.

caramel fudge coconut squares
Prepare the basic cookie dough and use caramel spread instead of jam.
Add 75 g (3 oz) chopped fudge pieces to the coconut topping.

cookies for kids

Kids love cookies – both eating them and making

them. This chapter is full of appealing ideas that

are accessible to both young and old. Encourage

your kids to read with alphabet cookies, make

gingerbread bears with your kids and let them

roll out the dough, or co-ordinate traffic jams

on the table!

fruit & nut refrigerator cookies

see variations page 113

These are likely to become a favourite with everyone who tries them.

450 g (1 lb) dark chocolate
225 g (8 oz) unsalted butter
300 g (10 oz) crumbled digestive biscuits

200 g (7 oz) toasted hazelnuts, chopped rough
150 g (5 oz) raisins
150 g (5 oz) halved red glacé cherries

Line a 23 x 33-cm (9 x 13-in) baking sheet with a layer of parchment.

Melt the chocolate and butter together in a large mixing bowl. Add the remaining ingredients. Stir thoroughly to ensure the ingredients are well mixed.

Spoon the mixture onto a lined baking sheet and level the surface with a palette knife. Cover and refrigerate for two to three hours or until firm enough to turn out and cut into wedges.

Store in the refrigerator for five to seven days.

Makes 2 dozen

pizza cookie

see variations page 114

A giant-size chewy cookie topped with cream cheese icing and brightly coloured sweets.
This would make a fun surprise for a child's party.

for the cookie

115 g (4 oz) unsalted butter
200 g (7 oz) caster sugar
1 egg
1 tsp vanilla essence
225 g (8 oz) plain flour
½ tsp bicarbonate of soda

for the topping

115 g (4 oz) unsalted butter
250 g (9 oz) icing sugar
115 g (4½ oz) cream cheese
150 g (5 oz) sweets
2 tbsp sugar strands

Pre-heat the oven to 175°C (350°F / Gas mark 4) and line a 30-cm (12-in) pizza tray or
baking sheet with parchment.

Beat the butter and caster sugar together. Then add the egg and vanilla essence. Sift the
flour and bicarbonate of soda and stir into the mixture. Spread the dough onto the pizza
tray or baking sheet. Bake for 18 to 20 minutes until golden. Remove from the oven and
allow to cool before transferring to a wire rack.

Beat the butter and icing sugar together and then beat in the cream cheese. Spread over
the cooled cookie and decorate with sweets and sugar strands.

Makes 1 large cookie

ice cream cookies

see variations page 115

For a fun dessert or party treat, pile up a whole lot of ice cream cookies on a plate, drizzle with fudge sauce and then sprinkle with sweets.

150 g (5 oz) plain flour
½ tsp bicarbonate of soda
50 g (2 oz) unsalted butter
50 g (2 oz) white vegetable fat
150 g (5 oz) caster sugar

1 egg
1 tsp vanilla essence
50 g (2 oz) cornflakes or crisped rice cereal
115 g (4 oz) melted plain chocolate
1 ltr (1¾ pt) vanilla ice cream

Pre-heat the oven to 175°C (350°F / Gas mark 4) and lightly grease two baking sheets. Sift the flour and bicarbonate of soda. Beat the butter and vegetable fat with the sugar until light and fluffy. Add the egg and vanilla essence and stir through the sifted flour and cereal.

Roll the dough into small balls. Place on baking sheets 5 cm (2 in) apart and flatten slightly. Bake for 8 to 10 minutes, then leave to cool on wire racks. Once completely cool, brush the cookie bases with melted chocolate and put them in the fridge to set for a few minutes. Spoon about 50 g (2 oz) of ice cream onto each cookie base and sandwich with the other cookie half.

Put the ice cream cookies in the freezer to harden, and then transfer to an airtight container in the freezer. Best eaten within four days.

Makes 1 dozen

peanut butter jam thumbprints

see variations page 116

With a thumbful of jam, these peanut butter delights will leave fingerprints all over the cookie jar.

150 g (5 oz) caster sugar
50 g (2 oz) light brown sugar
225 g (8 oz) peanut butter

1 egg
½ tsp vanilla essence
115 g (4 oz) raspberry jam

Pre-heat the oven to 190°C (375°F / Gas mark 5).

Combine all the ingredients in a large bowl, except the jam. Mix until smooth.

Roll the mixture into 2.5-cm (1-in) balls. If they are a bit sticky, use a little flour on your fingers.

Place the balls onto non-stick baking sheets about 5 cm (2 in) apart and, using a floured thumb, make a deep impression in each ball of dough. Bake for 10 to 12 minutes. Cool on a wire rack.

Fill each impression with jam. Store in an airtight container for four to five days.

Makes 3 dozen

gingerbread bears

see variations page 117

Gingerbread bears are great fun to make and decorate. Try piping names onto them and putting them in party bags for a child's party.

400 g (14 oz) plain flour
1 tsp bicarbonate of soda
1 tsp ground cinnamon
1½ tsp ground ginger
¼ tsp ground allspice
100 g (3½ oz) light brown sugar

4 tbsp treacle
1 egg
75 g (3 oz) melted unsalted butter
Royal icing to decorate
50 g (2 oz) sweets

Lightly grease two baking sheets. Sift the flour, bicarbonate of soda and spices together in a bowl. Add the sugar, treacle, egg and butter and mix to a smooth paste. Chill the dough until firm.

Pre-heat the oven to 190°C (375°F / Gas mark 5). Roll out the dough onto a lightly floured surface to 6 mm (¼ in) thick. Cut out the gingerbread bears using a floured cookie cutter.

Bake for 8 to 10 minutes. Cool on a wire rack. Decorate with royal icing. Use icing to affix the sweets.

Store in an airtight container for 7 to 10 days.

Makes 1 dozen

oat delights

see variations page 118

Very simple to make, oat delights are a great idea if the kids want to play chef and bake something on their own.

100 g (3½ oz) rolled oats
90 g (3¼ oz) flaked coconut
115 g (4 oz) plain chocolate, melted

25 g (1 oz) unsalted butter
2 tbsp golden syrup
3 tbsp Dutch process cocoa powder

Mix the oats and coconut together in a large bowl.

Melt the chocolate and butter and add the golden syrup. Pour the oats and coconut into the melted chocolate mixture and stir to combine.

Add the sifted Dutch process cocoa powder and stir to incorporate. Roll the mixture into balls. If the mix is too sticky, add a little more cocoa powder.

Refrigerate the balls on parchment-lined baking sheets. When they are firm, transfer to an airtight container in the refrigerator; they will keep for five to seven days.

Makes 1½ dozen

carnival bars

see variations page 119

For carnivals, birthdays or any other celebration, these bars are easy to package, pretty to serve and delicious to eat.

75 g (3 oz) unsalted butter
100 g (3½ oz) light brown sugar
1 egg
1 tsp vanilla essence

190 g (6½ oz) plain flour
½ tsp baking powder
100 g (3½ oz) sweets

Pre-heat the oven to 175°C (350°F / Gas mark 4). Line a 23-cm (9-in) square tin with parchment.

Beat the butter and sugar then add the egg and vanilla essence.

Sift the flour and baking powder and beat into the mixture. Stir in the sweets.

Press the mixture into the tin and bake for 20 to 25 minutes until golden brown. Cool in the tin and then cut into squares.

Store in an airtight container for five to seven days.

Makes 2 dozen

coconut & cherry macaroons

see variations page 120

These sweet treats are so addictive, it will be hard to stop at one.

175 g (6 oz) shredded coconut	2 tsp vanilla essence
4 egg whites	Pinch of salt
150 g (5 oz) caster sugar	75 g (3 oz) chopped red glacé cherries

Pre-heat the oven to 175°C (350°F / Gas mark 4). Line two baking sheets with parchment.

Combine all the ingredients except the cherries in a large heat-proof bowl over a pan of simmering water. Stir the mixture constantly for six minutes, or until the egg whites have started to thicken. The mixture is ready when its consistency is homogenous and holds shape.

Remove the bowl from the pan and stir in the cherries. Drop large spoonfuls of the mixture about 5 cm (2 in) apart on the lined baking sheets. Bake for 15 minutes until the macaroons are golden.

Slide the parchment and cookies onto wire racks and allow to cool completely.

Store in an airtight container for three to four days.

Makes 1½ dozen

blueberry & white chocolate crunchies

see variations page 121

Quick to make, but even quicker to eat, blueberries give these crunchies a tart twist.

450 g (1 lb) white chocolate, chopped
50 g (2 oz) unsalted butter
125 g (4½ oz) puffed rice cereal
150 g (5 oz) dried blueberries

Line a 23-cm (9-in) square tin with parchment.

Melt the chocolate and butter, then stir in the cereal and blueberries.

Spoon the mixture into the tin. Refrigerate until set and then cut into squares.

Store in an airtight container for five to seven days.

Makes 2 dozen

alphabet cookies

see variations page 122

Whet your child's appetite for spelling... cookie style!

175 g (6 oz) unsalted butter
200 g (7 oz) caster sugar
1½ tsp vanilla essence
375 g (13 oz) plain flour, sifted

1 egg
1 egg yolk
Royal icing, to decorate

Line two baking sheets with parchment. Blend the butter, sugar and vanilla essence in a food processor until smooth. Add the sifted flour, egg and egg yolk and process to a smooth dough. Wrap in parchment and refrigerate until firm.

Pre-heat the oven to 175°C (350°F / Gas mark 4). Roll out the dough either on a lightly floured work surface or between two sheets of parchment to 6 mm (¼ in) thick.

Cut out letters using cookie cutters or homemade stencils. Place the cookies on the sheets and bake for 10 to 12 minutes. Cool on wire racks.

Store in an airtight container for one week.

Makes 3 dozen

jammie dodgers

see variations page 123

Introducing the jammie dodger: every kid's favourite – every adult's soft spot.

300 g (10 oz) plain flour
50 g (2 oz) caster sugar
Pinch of salt
175 g (6 oz) unsalted butter

1 tsp vanilla essence
5 tbsp raspberry jam
2 tbsp icing sugar

Put the flour, sugar, salt, butter and vanilla essence in a food processor and blend until the mixture clumps. Work the dough into a flat round. Wrap in parchment and refrigerate until firm.

Pre-heat the oven to 175°C (350°F / Gas mark 4). Roll out the dough on a floured surface to 3 mm (⅛ in) thick. Cut out rounds using a 4-cm (1½-in) cookie cutter. Place half the cookies on parchment-lined baking sheets. Using a smaller round cutter, cut out the centres from the remaining cookies. Bake the cookies on separate baking sheets for 8 to 10 minutes, until golden.

Allow the cookies to cool before sandwiching together with jam. Make a small parchment piping bag, fill with jam and pipe more jam into the cut-out centres. Dust the cookies with icing sugar. Store unfilled cookies in an airtight container for a week, and filled cookies for three days.

Makes 2½ dozen

cookie cars

see variations page 124

You make the cookies, but let the kids design the cars. This recipe is a great project for a rainy afternoon, but be forewarned, there will be traffic jams on the table in no time.

190 g (6½ oz) plain flour
¼ tsp baking powder
Pinch of salt
115 g (4 oz) unsalted butter
150 g (5 oz) caster sugar

1 egg
1 tbsp milk
1 tsp vanilla essence
Royal icing, food colouring and sweets or silver
    balls to decorate

Sift the flour and baking powder, then add the salt. In a separate bowl, beat the butter and sugar until pale and fluffy, then beat in the egg, milk and vanilla essence.

Gradually add the flour mixture and mix to a smooth dough. Wrap in parchment and refrigerate until firm.

Pre-heat the oven to 200°C (400°F / Gas mark 6). Roll out the dough onto a lightly floured surface or between two sheets of parchment. Using a floured cutter, cut shapes from the dough. Place on non-stick baking sheets and bake for 8 to 10 minutes. Cool completely on wire racks. Decorate with royal icing.

Store in an airtight container for four to five days.

Makes 2 dozen

pecan chocolate mallow bars

see variations page 125

Crunchy, sticky chocolate bars to get your fingers and teeth stuck into. A great recipe to make with the kids – you do the melting and let them throw on the marshmallows.

75 g (3 oz) dark chocolate
115 g (4 oz) unsalted butter
200 g (7 oz) light brown sugar
2 eggs

75 g (3 oz) plain flour
1 tsp vanilla essence
100 g (3½ oz) chopped pecans
300 g (10 oz) large pink and white
    marshmallows

Preheat the oven to 175°C (350°F / Gas mark 4). Grease and line a 23-cm- (9-in-) square tin.

Melt the chocolate. Beat the butter and sugar until light and fluffy, then beat in the eggs. Stir in the sifted flour. Then stir in the melted chocolate, butter, vanilla and pecans.

Pour the mixture into the tin. Bake for 20 minutes, remove from the oven and cover with marshmallows. Return to the oven for 5 to 10 minutes until the marshmallows have melted.

Allow to cool in the tin and then refrigerate until completely cold before cutting into bars.

Store in an airtight container for five to seven days.

Makes 2 dozen

variations

fruit & nut refrigerator cookies

see base recipe page 91

fudge pecan refrigerator cookies
Prepare the basic cookie dough, substituting 200 g (7 oz) toasted chopped pecans for the hazelnuts, and 150 g (5 oz) chopped fudge for the glacé cherries.

ginger crunch refrigerator cookies
Prepare the basic cookie dough, using ginger snaps instead of digestive biscuits, and 3 tablespoons chopped crystallised ginger instead of the glacé cherries.

totally nuts refrigerator cookies
Prepare the basic cookie dough, using 200 g (7 oz) toasted chopped pecans instead of the raisins and cherries and stir in 4 tablespoons smooth peanut butter.

variations

pizza cookie

see base recipe page 92

ice cream pizza cookie
Prepare the basic cookie pizza. When the cookie has cooled, spread with 6 tablespoons chocolate-hazelnut spread. Top with scoops of vanilla, chocolate and strawberry ice cream and drizzle with chocolate sauce. Serve immediately.

marshmallow pizza cookie
Prepare the basic cookie pizza. When the cookie has cooled, spread with peanut butter and jam. Top with handfuls of miniature marshmallows.

tutti frutti pizza cookie
Prepare the basic cookie pizza. When the cookie has cooled, spread with whipped cream. Top with fresh fruits including strawberries, sliced bananas and blueberries.

variations

ice cream cookies

see base recipe page 95

mint-chocolate ice cream cookies
Prepare the basic cookie dough. Substitute 2 tablespoons Dutch process cocoa powder for an equal amount of the flour. Add 100 g (3½ oz) crushed mint sweets for the cereal. Fill the cookies with mint-chocolate ice cream.

nutty ice cream cookies
Prepare the basic cookie dough, then add 2 tablespoons smooth peanut butter and 50 g (2 oz) chopped pecans to the cookie mixture. Fill the cookies with caramel nut ice cream.

lemon & raspberry ice cream cookies
Prepare the basic cookie dough and add the grated zest of 2 lemons (4 to 6 teaspoons). Substitute white chocolate for the melted plain chocolate, and fill the cookies with raspberry or berry ripple ice cream.

variations

peanut butter jam thumbprints

see base recipe page 96

peanut butter, chocolate chip & jam thumbprints
Prepare the basic cookie dough and add 75 g (3 oz) dark chocolate chips to the dough.

peanut butter & chocolate thumbprints
Prepare the basic cookie dough and add 75 g (3 oz) dark chocolate chips to the dough. Fill the thumbprint impressions with chocolate-hazelnut spread.

peanut butter & cranberry thumbprints
Prepare the basic cookie dough and add 75 g (3 oz) dried cranberries and fill the thumbprint impressions with cranberry jelly.

variations

gingerbread bears

see base recipe page 99

raisin gingerbread bears
Prepare the basic cookie dough and add 75 g (3 oz) raisins. Bake
and decorate.

extra ginger gingerbread bears
Prepare the basic cookie dough and add 4 tablespoons chopped
crystallised ginger. Bake and decorate.

crunchy gingerbread bears
Prepare the basic cookie dough, then brush the cut-out gingerbread
bears with egg white and sprinkle with demerara sugar. Bake and decorate.

variations

oat delights

see base recipe page 100

cherry & oat delights
Prepare the basic cookie dough, adding 150 g (5 oz) chopped red
glacé cherries.

walnut oat delights
Prepare the basic cookie dough, adding 100 g (3½ oz) chopped walnuts.

peanut butter oat delights
Prepare the basic cookie dough, substituting 115 g (4 oz) smooth peanut
butter for the chocolate.

variations

carnival bars

see base recipe page 101

chocolate mint carnival bars
Prepare the basic cookie dough, substituting 2 tablespoons Dutch process cocoa powder for 2 tablespoons of the flour. Substitute peppermint essence for the vanilla essence and chocolate chips for the sweets.

peanut butter & caramel carnival bars
Prepare the basic cookie dough, adding 115 g (4 oz) peanut butter. Use caramel sweets.

fruity carnival bars
Prepare the basic cookie dough and substitute 75 g (3 oz) chopped red glacé cherries and 75 g (3 oz) chopped crystallised pineapple instead of the sweets.

variations

coconut & cherry macaroons

see base recipe page 103

chocolate chip macaroons
Prepare the basic cookie dough and substitute plain chocolate chips
for the cherries.

coconut & pineapple macaroons
Prepare the basic cookie dough and substitute 75 g (3 oz) chopped
crystallised pineapple for the cherries.

chocolate-dipped macaroons
Prepare the macaroons and when they are completely cool, half-dip
them in melted dark chocolate.

variations

blueberry & white chocolate crunchies

see base recipe page 104

chocolate nut & raisin crunchies
Prepare the basic cookie dough, substituting plain chocolate for the
white chocolate and 50 g (2 oz) chopped pecans and 75 g (3 oz) raisins
for the dried blueberries.

chocolate & cherry crunchies
Prepare the basic cookie dough, substituting dark chocolate for the white
chocolate and dried cherries for the blueberries.

chocolate mallow & strawberry crunchies
Prepare the basic cookie dough, then add 50 g (2 oz) miniature
marshmallows. Substitute dried strawberries for the blueberries.

variations

alphabet cookies

see base recipe page 107

candy alphabet cookies
Prepare the basic cookie dough and add 100 g (3½ oz) crushed sweets to the dough after removing it from the food processor and before chilling.

orange alphabet cookies
Prepare the basic cookie dough, adding the grated zest of 1 orange (2 to 3 teaspoons).

double-decker alphabet cookies
Prepare the basic cookie dough and cut out two of each letter. Bake and cool the cookies, then sandwich them together with your favourite icing. Dust the cookie tops with icing sugar or decorate with royal icing.

variations

jammie dodgers

see base recipe page 108

jammie dodgers with icing
Prepare the basic cookie recipe and bake. When the cookies have cooled, spread all of the cookie bases first with vanilla icing and then with fruit jam. Sandwich the halves together.

lemon jammie dodgers
Prepare the basic cookie recipe and bake, adding the grated zest of 1 lemon (2 to 3 teaspoons). When the cookies are cool, spread with lemon curd and lemon icing and sandwich the halves together.

maple jammie dodgers
Prepare the basic cookie dough, substituting 1 tablespoon maple syrup for 1 tablespoon of the caster sugar. When the cookies cool, fill with maple icing.

variations

cookie cars

see base recipe page 111

chocolate cookie cars
Prepare the basic cookie dough, substituting 2 tablespoons Dutch process cocoa powder for 2 tablespoons of the flour. Decorate with chocolate icing and sweets.

lemon & spice cookie cars
Prepare the basic cookie dough, then add the grated zest of 1 lemon (2 to 3 teaspoons) to the beaten butter and ½ teaspoon ground allspice to the sifted flour.

hazelnut cookie cars
Prepare the basic cookie dough, substituting 40 g (1½ oz) ground toasted hazelnuts for 40 g (1½ oz) flour.

pecan chocolate mallow bars

see base recipe page 112

peanut chocolate mallow bars
Prepare the basic cookie dough and add 50 g (2 oz) smooth peanut
butter to the mix. Substitute peanuts for the pecans.

cherry chocolate mallow bars
Prepare the basic cookie dough and substitute red glacé cherries
for the pecans.

orange chocolate walnut mallow bars
Prepare the basic cookie dough, adding the grated zest of 1 orange
(2 to 3 teaspoons) to the mix. Substitute walnuts for the pecans.

chocolate
cookies

White chocolate-chunk cookies, chocolate

shortbread, chocolate pinwheels, chewy chocolate

cookies, chocolate-dipped, drizzled and swirled –

this chapter is dunked in . . . chocolate, of course.

dalmatian bars

see variations page 147

These nutty chocolate bars are simple to make and, as their name suggests, are 'spotted' with chocolate and nuts.

150 g (5 oz) dark chocolate
175 g (6 oz) unsalted butter
4 eggs
350 g (12 oz) caster sugar
2 tsp vanilla essence

190 g (6½ oz) plain flour
1 tsp baking powder
¼ tsp salt
150 g (5 oz) macadamia nuts
175 g (6 oz) white chocolate chips

Pre-heat the oven to 190°C (375°F / Gas mark 5). Grease and line a 23 x 33-cm (9 x 13-in) tin with parchment.

Melt the chocolate and the butter together. Beat the eggs and sugar with the vanilla and stir into the chocolate mixture. Stir in the sifted dry ingredients, and lastly, stir in the macadamia nuts and three-quarters of the chocolate chips.

Spoon into the prepared tin, level the surface and sprinkle with the remaining chocolate chips. Bake for 20 to 25 minutes or until firm. Cool in the tin and cut into bars.

Store in an airtight container for four to five days.

Makes 2 dozen

cream cheese & chocolate double deckers

see variations page 148

Crumbly cookies filled with a sweet cream cheese – simply luxurious.

150 g (5 oz) plain flour
½ tsp bicarbonate of soda
225 g (8 oz) cream cheese
50 g (2 oz) unsalted butter
150 g (5 oz) caster sugar

1 egg
100 g (3½ oz) dark chocolate, melted

for the filling

125 g (4½ oz) icing sugar

Pre-heat the oven to 175°C (350°F / Gas mark 4). Sift the flour and bicarbonate of soda and set aside. Beat half of the cream cheese and the butter until soft and smooth, then add the sugar and egg and beat until light and fluffy. Stir in the chocolate and then the sifted flour mixture. Mix to a smooth dough. Drop spoonfuls of dough onto baking sheets and bake for 10 to 12 minutes until firm at the edges. Remove from the sheets onto wire racks and allow to cool.

Beat the remaining cream cheese and sifted icing sugar until soft and smooth, and spread on the bases of half of the cookies. Sandwich with the remaining halves.

When completely cool, store in an airtight container in the fridge for two to three days.

Makes 2 dozen

white chocolate chunk cookies

see variations page 149

For all those white chocolate fans – this one's for you.

115 g (4 oz) unsalted butter
200 g (7 oz) caster sugar
1 egg
2 tsp vanilla essence
190 g (6½ oz) plain flour
½ tsp bicarbonate of soda

½ tsp baking powder
¼ tsp salt
50 g (2 oz) oatmeal
225 g (8 oz) chopped white
    chocolate chunks

Preheat the oven to 190°C (375°F / Gas mark 5). Beat the butter and sugar and then add the egg and vanilla. Sift together the dry ingredients and stir in the oatmeal. Incorporate the mixed dry ingredients and chocolate into the butter mixture.

Roll into balls and use your fingers to flatten onto a non-stick baking sheet 5 cm (2 in) apart. Bake for 8 to 10 minutes. Cool for five minutes.

When cool, store in an airtight container for four to five days.

Makes 2 dozen

chocolate-drizzled ginger cookies

see variations page 150

Crisp, spicy and drizzled with dark chocolate, this is a more sophisticated cookie.

1 egg
1 egg yolk
200 g (7 oz) caster sugar
115 g (4 oz) unsalted butter, melted
340 g (11½ oz) plain flour
¼ tsp bicarbonate of soda

1½ tsp ground ginger
¼ tsp salt

for the topping

6 oz dark chocolate, melted

Grease two baking sheets. Mix together the egg, egg yolk and sugar and then stir in the melted butter. Sift the flour, bicarbonate of soda, ginger and salt into a bowl. Add the dry ingredients to the egg mixture and mix to combine. Chill the dough until firm.

Pre-heat the oven to 190°C (375°F / Gas mark 5). Roll the dough out between parchment or cling film to 3 mm (⅛ in) thick. Cut out 5-cm (2-in) rounds and lay them on baking sheets. Bake for 15 minutes until golden. Cool on a wire rack. Dip a fork in the melted chocolate, drizzle chocolate over each cookie and place on parchment for the chocolate to set. Store in an airtight container for five to seven days.

Makes 2 dozen

marbled chocolate & vanilla cookies

see variations page 151

These attractive little cookies will go perfectly with your afternoon coffee.

375 g (13 oz) plain flour
100 g (3½ oz) icing sugar
250 g (9 oz) unsalted butter
2 tbsp double cream

2 tsp vanilla essence
3 tbsp Dutch process cocoa powder
1 egg white
2 tbsp granulated sugar

Grease two baking sheets. Sift the flour and icing sugar together and rub in the butter.

When the mixture starts to come together, add the cream and vanilla essence. Divide the mixture in half and add the sifted cocoa powder to one half. Knead the separate doughs lightly until smooth. Mix small amounts of each dough together and roll into four 4-cm- (1½-in-) wide logs. Wrap in parchment and refrigerate until firm.

Pre-heat the oven to 190°C (375°F / Gas mark 5). Brush each log with egg white and roll in granulated sugar. Cut into 6-mm (¼-in) thick slices. Place the cookie slices on the baking sheets and bake for 8 to 10 minutes. Cool on a wire rack.

When completely cool, store in an airtight container for five to seven days.

Makes 3½ dozen

chocolate shortbread

see variations page 152

Rich shortbread with a chocolate twist – use this recipe as a base for cheesecakes or for other desserts, or on its own with a large glass of milk.

200 g (7 oz) plain flour
6 tbsp Dutch process cocoa powder
¼ tsp salt
100 g (3½ oz) caster sugar

175 g (6 oz) unsalted butter
2 tsp vanilla essence
2 tsp granulated sugar

Pre-heat the oven to 150˚C (300˚F / Gas mark 2). Line an 18 x 28-cm (7 x 11-in) tin with foil.

Sift the flour and cocoa powder into a large bowl and add the salt. Beat the butter and sugar. Add the vanilla essence and stir in the dry ingredients. Knead the dough until it starts to clump together and then press into the tin.

Bake for 45 to 50 minutes. The shortbread will look cooked before it actually is, so ensure that it is baked for the full amount of time.

Remove from the oven, sprinkle with granulated sugar and cut into fingers. Leave to cool for 20 minutes before removing from the tin. Store in an airtight container for up to five days.

Makes 1½ dozen

chocolate spice cookies

see variations page 153

These full-flavoured cookies need to be covered in quality dark chocolate for the best results.

190 g (6½ oz) plain flour
2 tbsp cocoa powder
½ tsp baking powder
½ tsp ground allspice
Pinch of salt

50 g (2 oz) unsalted butter
150 g (5 oz) light brown sugar
1 egg
3 tbsp maple syrup

Line two baking sheets with parchment.

Sift the flour, cocoa powder, baking powder, spices and salt in a bowl. In a separate bowl, beat the butter and sugar until light and fluffy, then beat in the egg. Stir in the maple syrup and then add the dry ingredients. Wrap and refrigerate until firm.

Pre-heat the oven to 190°C (375°F / Gas mark 5). Roll out the dough equally between two sheets of cling film. Peel off the cling film and cut the dough with a floured 5-cm (2-in) cutter. Put the cookies on the baking sheets and chill until firm. Remove from the refrigerator and bake for 8 to 10 minutes. Slide the parchment onto wire racks to cool.

When completely cool, store in an airtight container for five to seven days.

Makes 2½ dozen

chocolate & orange sandwich cookies

see variations page 154

Chocolate and orange is a great flavour combination. Try these cookies and you'll see why.

for the cookies

225 g (8 oz) dark chocolate, coarsely chopped
50 g (2 oz) plain flour
¼ tsp baking powder
Pinch of salt
2 eggs
100 g (3½ oz) caster sugar
Grated zest of 1 orange (2 to 3 tsp)

for the filling

75 g (3 oz) unsalted butter
125 g (4½ oz) icing sugar
Grated zest (2 to 3 tsp) and juice
(3 tbsp) of 1 orange

Pre-heat the oven to 175°C (350°F / Gas mark 4). Line two baking sheets with parchment. Melt the chocolate and allow it to cool slightly. Sift the flour, baking powder and salt together in another bowl. Whisk the eggs, sugar and orange zest, and stir into the melted chocolate. Stir in the flour. Spoon small amounts of the dough onto the baking sheets 5 cm (2 in) apart. Bake for 10 to 25 minutes. Slide the parchment onto cooling racks.

Beat the filling ingredients together until fluffy. Spread the icing on the base of a cookie and sandwich with another. Store the cookies in an airtight container for four to five days.

Makes 1½ dozen

chocolate pinwheels

see variations page 155

Great favourites both to make and eat – and they look so very impressive.

100 g (3½ oz) dark chocolate, coarsely chopped
375 g (13 oz) plain flour
2 tsp baking powder
¼ tsp salt

115 g (4 oz) unsalted butter
125 g (4½ oz) caster sugar
2 eggs
2 tsp vanilla essence

Line two baking sheets with parchment. Melt the chocolate and allow to cool slightly. Sift the flour, baking powder and salt together in another bowl. In a separate bowl, beat butter and sugar until soft and creamy, then add the eggs and vanilla essence. Stir the dry ingredients into the butter mixture to form a smooth paste. Divide the mix between two bowls. Mix the chocolate into one half of the dough. Wrap in parchment and refrigerate until firm.

Roll out the chocolate dough on floured parchment and brush off any excess flour. Roll out the plain dough on another sheet of parchment and lay the plain dough on top of the chocolate dough. Roll lightly with the rolling pin and trim the long edges. Roll up the dough tightly from the longer side. Wrap in parchment and refrigerate until firm. Pre-heat the oven to 190°C (375°F / Gas mark 5). Slice thinly and lay on baking sheets. Bake for 8 to 10 minutes. Cool on a wire rack, and store in an airtight container for five to seven days.

Makes 3 dozen

chocolate fingers

see variations page 156

Richly flavoured chocolate fingers are a tempting treat for the entire family.

150 g (5 oz) plain chocolate
115 g (4 oz) unsalted butter
225 g (8 oz) cream cheese
150 g (5 oz) caster sugar
1 egg

1 tsp vanilla essence
300 g (10 oz) plain flour
½ tsp baking powder
50 g (2 oz) white chocolate chips
75 g (3 oz) coarsely chopped toasted pecans

Pre-heat the oven to 190°C (375°F / Gas mark 5). Line a 23 x 33-cm (9 x 13-in) tin.

Melt the chocolate. Beat the butter, cream cheese, sugar, egg and vanilla essence until soft and smooth. Sift the flour and baking powder and stir into the butter mixture. Spread the mixture into the tin and level the surface. Bake for 15 to 20 minutes until firm.

Remove from the oven, drizzle the melted chocolate over the top and sprinkle with the remaining ingredients. Allow to cool and set, then cut into fingers.

Store in an airtight container for five to seven days.

Makes 2 dozen

chewy chocolate cookies

see variations page 157

Simply irresistible cookies, perfect for any time of day.

175 g (6 oz) dark chocolate, chopped
50 g (2 oz) unsalted butter
50 g (2 oz) plain flour
¼ tsp baking powder
Pinch of salt

2 eggs
250 g (9 oz) caster sugar
1 tsp vanilla essence
115 g (4 oz) plain chocolate, chopped

Pre-heat the oven to 180°C (350°F / Gas mark 4). Line two baking sheets with parchment.

Melt the dark chocolate and butter. Allow to cool slightly. Sift the flour, baking powder and salt together. In another bowl, beat the eggs, sugar and vanilla essence until thick and pale. Stir the melted chocolate into the eggs and sugar, followed by the flour and plain chocolate chunks.

Drop tablespoons of the mixture onto the baking sheets and bake for 8 to 10 minutes. Slide the parchment onto wire racks.

When completely cool, store in an airtight container for two to three days.

Makes 2 dozen

chocolate whirls

see variations page 158

Pretty little cookies that taste as good as they look.

for the cookies

225 g (8 oz) softened unsalted butter
50 g (2 oz) icing sugar
25 g (1 oz) dark chocolate, melted
225 g (8 oz) plain flour
2 tbsp Dutch process cocoa powder
3 tbsp cornflour

for the filling

50 g (2 oz) unsalted butter
190 g (6½ oz) icing sugar
25 g (1 oz) dark chocolate, melted
2 tbsp icing sugar

Pre-heat the oven to 175°C (350°F / Gas mark 4). Beat the butter and icing sugar together until light and fluffy. Stir in the chocolate. Sift the flour, cocoa powder and cornflour and stir into the creamed mixture.

Pipe the mixture using a 1½-cm (¾-in) fluted nozzle into 5-cm (2-in) rosettes spaced 5 cm (2 in) apart on a non-stick baking sheet. Bake for 10 to 12 minutes until golden. Allow to firm up slightly before transferring them to a wire rack to cool. Beat the butter and icing sugar together until light and fluffy and stir in the chocolate. Spread the filling onto the bottom of half the cookies, and then sandwich together with the other halves. Dust with the 2 tablespoons of icing sugar. Store filled cookies in an airtight container for three to four days and unfilled cookies for five to seven days.

Makes 1½ dozen

triple chocolate cookies

see variations page 159

Rich and full-flavoured, these chunky chocolate cookies with dark and white chocolate chips are irresistible.

150 g (5 oz) plain flour
50 g (2 oz) unsweetened cocoa powder
½ tsp bicarbonate of soda
¼ tsp baking powder
Pinch of salt
115 g (4 oz) unsalted butter

100 g (3½ oz) granulated sugar
100 g (3½ oz) light brown sugar
1 egg
1 tsp vanilla essence
100 g (3½ oz) plain chocolate chips
100 g (3½ oz) white chocolate chips

Pre-heat the oven to 160°C (350°F / Gas mark 4). Sift together the flour, cocoa powder, bicarbonate of soda, baking powder and salt. Set aside. Beat the butter and sugar until smooth and creamy and beat in the egg and vanilla essence. Add the flour mixture and mix until almost blended. Add the chocolate chips and mix.

Scoop the dough onto a baking sheet 5 cm (2 in) apart. If preparing dough ahead, roll the dough into a log 4 cm (1½ in) thick, wrap in foil and refrigerate for two hours. Before baking, cut the log into 6-mm (¼-in) slices and place the slices 4 cm (1½ in) apart on a non-stick baking sheet. Bake for 12 to 14 minutes.

Transfer to a wire rack to coo,l and store in an airtight container for five to seven days.

Makes 3 dozen

dalmatian bars

see base recipe page 127

cherry dalmatian bars
Prepare the basic cookie dough and substitute 75 g (3 oz) whole glacé
cherries for 75 g (3 oz) of the white chocolate chips.

double chocolate dalmatian bars
Prepare the basic cookie dough and substitute 75 g (3 oz) milk chocolate for
the dark chocolate.

chocolate orange dalmatian bars
Prepare the basic cookie dough and add the grated zest of 1 orange
(2 to 3 teaspoons) to the butter and sugar mixture.

variations

cream cheese & chocolate double deckers

see base recipe page 128

cream cheese, walnut & chocolate double deckers
Prepare the basic cookie dough and add 75 g (3 oz) coarsely chopped walnuts to the mixture.

cream cheese & white chocolate double deckers
Prepare the basic cookie dough and add 75 g (3 oz) white chocolate chips to the mixture.

cream cheese, raisin & chocolate double deckers
Prepare the basic cookie dough and add 75 g (3 oz) raisins to the mixture.

variations

white chocolate-chunk cookies

see base recipe page 131

white chocolate-chunk & raisin cookies
Prepare the basic cookie dough and add 75 g (3 oz) raisins with the white chocolate chunks.

dark-dipped white chocolate-chunk cookies
Prepare the basic cookie dough. When the cookies are baked and cool, dip half of each cookie in melted chocolate and place on parchment until the chocolate is set.

white chocolate-chunk & pecan cookies
Prepare the basic cookie dough and add 75 g (3 oz) chopped pecans with the white chocolate chunks.

variations

chocolate-drizzled ginger cookies

see base recipe page 132

lemon chocolate-dipped cookies
Prepare the basic cookie dough, substituting the grated zest of 2 lemons
(4 to 6 teaspoons) for the ground ginger. Add the lemon zest to the egg
and sugar mixture.

cinnamon chocolate-dipped cookies
Prepare the basic cookie dough, substituting ground cinnamon for the
ground ginger.

vanilla chocolate-dipped cookies
Prepare the basic cookie dough, substituting 2 teaspoons vanilla essence
for the ground ginger.

marbled chocolate & vanilla cookies

see base recipe page 135

chocolate orange-marbled cookies
Prepare the basic cookie dough, then add the grated zest of 1 orange
(2 to 4 teaspoons) and ⅛ teaspoon orange food colouring to one half of
the dough. Marble the doughs together in the same way.

chocolate mint-marbled cookies
Prepare the basic cookie dough, then add ⅛ teaspoon green food colouring
and add ¼ teaspoon peppermint essence to one half of the dough. Marble
the doughs together in the same way.

chocolate raspberry-marbled cookies
Prepare the basic cookie dough, then add ⅛ teaspoon red food colouring
and ¼ teaspoon raspberry flavour to one half of the dough. Marble the
doughs together in the same way.

variations

chocolate shortbread

see base recipe page 136

chocolate & orange shortbread
Prepare the basic cookie dough, adding the grated zest of 1 orange
(2 to 3 teaspoons) to the butter and sugar.

chocolate chip shortbread
Prepare the basic cookie dough, adding 100 g (3½ oz) plain chocolate chips
when the dough starts to clump together.

chocolate & ginger shortbread
Prepare the basic cookie dough, adding 3 tablespoons chopped crystallised
ginger when the dough starts to clump together.

variations

chocolate spice cookies

see base recipe page 137

chocolate pecan spice cookies
Prepare the basic cookie dough and add 75 g (3 oz) coarsely chopped pecans.

chocolate cinnamon maple cookies
Prepare the basic cookie dough and substitute cinnamon for the allspice.

chocolate ginger cookies
Prepare the basic cookie dough and substitute ground ginger for the allspice, and treacle for the maple syrup.

chocolate & orange sandwich cookies

see base recipe page 139

chocolate & orange sandwich cookies with vanilla cream filling
Prepare the basic cookie dough and substitute 2 teaspoons vanilla essence for the grated orange zest and juice in the filling.

chocolate & orange sandwich cookies with mocha filling
Prepare the basic cookie dough and substitute 2 teaspoons instant coffee powder for the grated orange zest and juice in the filling. Dissolve the coffee in 1 tablespoon hot water first.

chocolate mint sandwich cookies with chocolate filling
Prepare the basic cookie dough, then substitute ¼ teaspoon peppermint essence for the grated orange zest in the cookies and 1 tablespoon Dutch process cocoa powder dissolved in 1 tablespoon hot water for the grated orange zest and juice in the filling.

variations

chocolate pinwheels

see base recipe page 140

mocha pinwheels
Prepare the basic cookie dough, adding the chocolate to one half of the
dough and 2 teaspoons instant coffee powder dissolved in 1 tablespoon
hot water to the other half.

raspberry & lemon pinwheels
Prepare the basic cookie dough, substituting 2 teaspoons raspberry
flavour and ½ teaspoon pink food colouring for the chocolate in one
half of the dough. In the other half, add the grated zest of 1 lemon
(2 to 3 teaspoons) and ½ teaspoon yellow food colouring.

chocolate & lemon pinwheels
Prepare the basic cookie dough, adding the chocolate to one half of the
dough and grated zest of 1 lemon (2 to 3 teaspoons) and ½ teaspoon
yellow food colouring to the other half.

variations

chocolate fingers

see base recipe page 141

mega chocolate fingers
Prepare the basic cookie dough, substituting 2 tablespoons cocoa powder for an equal amount of the flour. Add 75 g (3 oz) milk chocolate chips into the mixture before spreading it into the tin.

peanut chocolate fingers
Prepare the basic cookie dough, substituting 2 tablespoons cocoa powder for an equal amount of the flour and stir in all the melted chocolate. When baked, spread with 225 g (8 oz) smooth peanut butter and top with the pecans and 75 g (3 oz) butterscotch chips.

chocolate banana fingers
Prepare the basic cookie dough and add 1 mashed banana to the mixture. Bake and top with the pecans and 75 g (3 oz) banana chips.

chewy chocolate cookies

see base recipe page 142

chewy chocolate walnut cookies
Prepare the basic cookie dough and add 75 g (3 oz) coarsely
chopped walnuts.

chewy chocolate cherry cookies
Prepare the basic cookie dough and add 75 g (3 oz) chopped natural
glacé cherries.

chewy chocolate & raisin cookies
Prepare the basic cookie dough and add 75 g (3 oz) raisins.

variations

chocolate whirls

see base recipe page 145

dipped chocolate whirls
Prepare the basic cookie dough and then half-dip the filled cookies in melted dark chocolate.

chocolate & ginger whirls
Prepare the basic cookie dough, adding 1 teaspoon ground ginger to the flour and 2 tablespoons chopped crystallised ginger to the filling.

chocolate cinnamon & raisin whirls
Prepare the basic cookie dough, adding 1 teaspoon ground cinnamon to the flour and 2 tablespoons raisins to the filling.

triple chocolate cookies

see base recipe page 146

peppermint chocolate chip cookies
Prepare the basic dark cookie dough using half the quantity of cocoa powder. Add ¼ teaspoon peppermint essence and 200 g (7 oz) plain chocolate chips.

walnut chip cookies
Prepare the basic dark cookie dough using half the quantity of cocoa powder, then add 100 g (3½ oz) chopped walnuts and 100 g (3½ oz) plain chocolate chips.

dark chocolate cherry cookies
Prepare the basic dark cookie dough. Add 100 g (3½ oz) chopped glacé cherries and 100 g (3½ oz) dark chocolate chips.

celebration cookies

Cookies are an ideal way to mark a special occasion – use these recipes to concoct heart-shaped cookies for Valentine's Day, fortune cookies to see in the Chinese New Year, or to bake traditional Rugelach and Christmas shortbread.

christmas tree cookies

see variations page 182

These cookies are a great – and inexpensive – festive gift idea.

190 g (6½ oz) plain flour
½ tsp baking powder
Pinch of salt
115 g (4 oz) unsalted butter
100 g (3½ oz) caster sugar

1 egg
1 tsp vanilla essence
1 egg white
3 tbsp green sugar crystals
Royal icing and sweets, to decorate

Pre-heat the oven to 160°C (350°F / Gas mark 4). Sift the flour, baking powder and salt together. Beat the butter and sugar until smooth, add the egg and vanilla essence and stir in the dry ingredients. Mix the dough with your hands.

Put 50 g (2 oz) of dough aside and divide the remainder in half. Roll into two logs about 5 cm (2 in) thick. Gently press each log into a triangular shape. Wrap and refrigerate the logs and the extra dough until firm. Cut the triangular logs into 6-mm- (¼-in-) thick slices and lay them 5 cm (2 in) apart on baking sheets. Mould the excess dough into tree-trunk shapes and attach to achieve a Christmas tree shape. Alternately, use a tree-shaped cookie cutter.

Brush each Christmas tree cookie with egg white and sprinkle with the sugar crystals. Bake for 8 to 10 minutes until golden. Remove onto wire racks and allow to cool. Decorate with royal icing and sweets. Store in an airtight container for four to five days.

Makes 1 dozen

cinnamon stars

see variations page 183

These cookies can be made to accompany almost any celebration – just change the decoration according to the occasion.

200 g (7 oz) ground almonds
1 tsp ground cinnamon
200 g (7 oz) caster sugar
½ egg white

2 tbsp icing sugar, to dust
    work surface
Royal icing, sweets and coloured sugar crystals
    to decorate

Pre-heat the oven to 150°C (300°F / Gas mark 2). Line two baking sheets with parchment. Mix together the ground almonds, cinnamon and sugar. Add the egg white and water, and work to a smooth dough with your hands.

Roll out the dough on a surface dusted with icing sugar to 6 mm (¼ in) thick. Cut out stars using a star-shaped cookie cutter. Place the cookies on the baking sheets and bake for 30 to 35 minutes.

Transfer to wire racks and allow to cool. Pipe or spread with royal icing and decorate with sweets and coloured sugar crystals.

Makes 1½ dozen

easter chocolate nest cookies

see variations page 184

Kids will love these and they taste as good as they look!

115 g (4 oz) unsalted butter
100 g (3½ oz) caster sugar
100 g (3½ oz) demerera sugar
2 eggs
1 tsp vanilla essence
2 tbsp dark chocolate, melted
200 g (7 oz) plain flour

2 tbsp Dutch process cocoa powder
¼ tsp bicarbonate of soda
Pinch of salt
90 g (3¼ oz) flaked coconut
75 g (3 oz) rolled oats
200 g (7 oz) miniature chocolate eggs

Pre-heat the oven to 160°C (350°F / Gas mark 4). Grease two baking sheets. Beat the butter and sugars. Add the eggs, vanilla essence and melted chocolate and beat until smooth.

Sift the flour, Dutch process cocoa powder, bicarbonate of soda and salt together and stir into the butter mixture. Stir the coconut and oats into the mixture and mix to combine. Drop spoonfuls onto baking sheets and shape into small rounds about 5 cm (2 in) in diameter. Using a floured thumb, make a 2 cm (1 in) impression in each cookie. Bake for 10 to 12 minutes.

Transfer to wire racks to cool. When completely cool, fill with the miniature chocolate eggs. Store in an airtight container for four to five days.

Makes 2 dozen

valentine heart cookies

see variations page 185

For a sweeter valentine gift, make personalised valentine cookies instead of cards.

175 g (6 oz) unsalted butter
200 g (7 oz) icing sugar
1½ tsp vanilla essence
375 g (13 oz) plain flour

1 egg
1 egg yolk
Royal icing, red and pink food colouring, to
    decorate

Line two baking sheets with parchment. Combine the butter, sugar and vanilla essence in a food processor until smooth.

Add the sifted flour, and the egg and egg yolk and process to a smooth dough. Wrap in parchment and refrigerate until firm.

Pre-heat the oven to 175°C (350°F / Gas mark 4). Roll out the dough either on a lightly floured work surface or between two sheets of parchment to 6 mm (¼ in) thick.

Cut out cookies using heart-shaped cutters. Place the cookies on the sheets and bake for 10 to 12 minutes. Cool on wire racks. Decorate with the royal icing. Store in an airtight container for five to seven days.

Makes 2 dozen

lovers' knots

see variations page 186

Not just for lovers! Make these for friends and family – they're sure to be appreciated.

150 g (5 oz) plain flour
½ tsp baking powder
Pinch of salt
15 g (½ oz) unsalted butter
2 tbsp caster sugar

Grated zest of 1 lemon
1 egg
1½ tbsp rum
2 tbsp icing sugar

Sift the flour, baking powder and salt into a bowl. Rub in the butter and then add the sugar and lemon zest. Stir in the egg and rum, and work the mixture until it forms a smooth dough. Turn onto a floured surface and knead the dough. Cover and let stand for 30 minutes.

Divide the dough in half, cover one half in parchment and roll out the other half to 31 x 8 cm (12 x 3 in). Cut the rectangle into 1-cm (½-in) strips and tie each strip loosely into a knot. Put to one side and repeat using the remaining dough.

Heat a deep fat fryer to 190°C (375°F) and deep-fry the dough in small batches until golden. Remove with a slotted spoon, drain on kitchen paper and dust with icing sugar. Serve while still warm.

Makes 2 dozen

lebkuchen

see variations page 187

Classic German spiced honey biscuits are very popular, especially at Christmas time.

for the cookies

1 egg
150 g (5 oz) light brown sugar
125 ml (4 fl oz) honey
125 ml (4 fl oz) treacle
450 g (1 lb) plain flour
1¼ tsp ground nutmeg
1¼ tsp ground cinnamon
½ tsp ground cloves
½ tsp ground allspice

for the glaze

190 g (6½ oz) icing sugar
1 tbsp egg white
1 tbsp lemon juice
Grated zest of 1 lemon

Grease three baking sheets. Beat the egg and sugar together until light and fluffy. Stir in the honey and treacle. Sift the flour and spices and stir into the egg mixture. Chill until firm, for about two hours or overnight. Pre-heat the oven to 160°C (350°F / Gas mark 4). Roll out to 6 mm (¼ in) thick, and cut into three 8 x 5 cm (3 x 2 in) rectangles. Bake for 10 to 12 minutes.

Transfer to a wire rack. Mix the icing sugar, egg white, lemon juice and lemon zest together and brush this glaze over the cookies. Allow the glaze to firm, then store the cookies in an airtight container for four to five days.

Makes 1½ dozen

rugelach

see variations page 188

These Jewish pastries are classic cookies for the festival of Channukah. Make sure the kitchen isn't too warm when you're making the dough or it may prove troublesome.

for the cookies

225 g (8 oz) unsalted butter
225 g (8 oz) cream cheese
375 g (13 oz) plain flour

for the filling

150 g (5 oz) caster sugar
75 g (3 oz) raisins
1 tsp ground cinnamon
100 g (3½ oz) ground almonds

Beat the butter and cream cheese together until smooth. Beat in the flour a little at a time. Knead the dough lightly until the flour is incorporated. Refrigerate until the dough is firm. While the dough is chilling, make the filling. Mix together 100 g (3½ oz) of the sugar, the raisins, cinnamon and almonds. Roll out half the dough between two pieces of lightly floured cling film. Work quickly, as the dough becomes hard to manage as it warms up. Roll to a rectangle and cut triangles the size of pie wedges from the dough, with the sides slightly longer than the base. Repeat with the remaining half of the dough.

Pre-heat the oven to 175°C (350°F / Gas mark 4). Spread a little of the filling on top of the dough wedges and roll up towards the point. Place on baking sheets with the point tucked under the roll. Sprinkle with sugar and bake for 15 to 18 minutes until golden. Serve hot or cold. Store in an airtight container for three to five days.

Makes 3 dozen

giant pumpkin cookies

see variations page 189

Ghosts, witches and cats are all part of Hallowe'en – and now so are pumpkin cookies.

for the cookies

265 g (9½ oz) plain flour
1 tsp baking powder
½ tsp salt
115 g (4 oz) unsalted butter
100 g (3½ oz) caster sugar
2 eggs
1 tsp vanilla essence

for the icing

250 g (9 oz) icing sugar
4 tbsp milk
Orange and black food colouring
Royal icing, to decorate
Orange and green sugar crystals

Pre-heat the oven to 175°C (350°F / Gas mark 4). Sift the flour, baking powder and salt together in a bowl. In a separate bowl, beat the butter and sugar and add the eggs and vanilla essence. Stir the dry ingredients to form a smooth dough. Wrap the dough in parchment and refrigerate until firm.

Cut the dough in half and roll out each piece on a lightly floured sheet of parchment to 6 mm (¼ in) thick. Cut out a large pumpkin shape either freehand, or use a stencil cut from thickened card or plastic. Lift onto a baking sheet. Bake for 12 to 15 minutes until golden. Cool on the baking sheet and transfer to a wire rack. When completely cool, combine the icing ingredients and decorate. Store in an airtight container for five to seven days.

Makes 2 to 4

layered birthday cookie

see variations page 190

Create your own extravagant birthday alternative for a cookie lover.

for the cookie

225 g (8 oz) unsalted butter
400 g (14 oz) light brown sugar
2 eggs
2 tsp vanilla essence
450 g (1 lb) plain flour
6 tbsp Dutch process cocoa powder
1 tsp bicarbonate of soda

for the topping

115 g (4 oz) unsalted butter
250 g (9 oz) icing sugar
225 g (8 oz) cream cheese
115 g (4 oz) melted dark chocolate
75 g (3 oz) sweets
75 g (3 oz) plain chocolate chips

Pre-heat the oven to 175°C (350°F / Gas mark 4). Line two 28-cm (11-in) springform tins with parchment. Beat the butter and sugar together. Add the eggs and vanilla essence. Sift the flour, Dutch process cocoa powder and bicarbonate of soda and stir into the mixture. Divide the dough into two and press into the prepared tins. Bake for 20 minutes until golden. Remove from the oven and allow to cool, then transfer to a wire rack.

To prepare the topping, beat the butter and icing sugar together, then beat in the cream cheese and melted chocolate. Spread the topping over the cooled cookies, place one on top of the other, decorate and top with the sweets and chocolate chips.

Makes 1 large cookie

witches' hats

see variations page 191

For visiting ghosts and ghouls on All Hallows' Eve.

300 g (10 oz) plain flour	200 g (7 oz) caster sugar
½ tsp baking powder	1 egg
Pinch of salt	2 tsp vanilla essence
115 g (4 oz) unsalted butter	Royal icing and food colouring, to decorate

Line two baking sheets with parchment. Sift the flour, baking powder and salt into a bowl. In a separate bowl, beat the butter and sugar until light and fluffy. Add the egg and vanilla. Stir in the flour mixture until incorporated and knead lightly until combined. Divide the dough in half, flatten each half into a patty, wrap in parchment and refrigerate until firm.

Pre-heat the oven to 175°C (350°F / Gas mark 4). Roll out the dough between two lightly floured sheets of cling film or parchment to 3 mm (⅛ in) thick. Using a floured witch's hat cutter or a plastic stencil, cut out cookies and put onto the baking sheets 4 cm (1½ in) apart. Bake for 8 to 10 minutes.

Slide the parchment onto wire racks and allow the cookies to cool. Decorate with royal icing.

Store in an airtight container for five to seven days.

Makes 2 dozen

fortune cookies

see variations page 192

Write your own fortunes and enclose them in the fold of these crunchy Chinese cookies.

2 to 3 egg whites
100 g (3½ oz) caster sugar
Pinch of salt
¼ tsp vanilla essence

150 g (5oz) plain flour
Pinch of ground star anise
115 g (4 oz) melted unsalted butter
2 tbsp water

Line two baking sheets with parchment. Beat together the egg whites, sugar and salt. Stir in the vanilla, flour and star anise. Add the butter and water and mix to a smooth paste.

Refrigerate for about 30 minutes until the mixture is set. Pre-heat the oven to 175°C (350°F / Gas mark 4). Spread small amounts of the mixture onto the parchment to form 8-cm (3-in) circles, 4 cm (1½ in) apart. Bake for three to four minutes until the edges start to brown.

Carefully remove one cookie at a time with a palette knife. Turn upside down, place a fortune paper inside and fold in half. Pinch in the middle and fold again to give a fortune cookie shape. Put to one side to cool and harden. If they become too hard, return the cookies to the oven for a few seconds. Store in an airtight container for five to seven days.

Makes 2 dozen

gumdrop party cookies

see variations page 193

These are the Martini of the cookie world – any time, any place, anywhere – just decorate with different coloured gumdrops. For Christmas, use red and green, and for Hallowe'en, orange and black.

350 g (12 oz) plain flour
1 tsp bicarbonate of soda
Pinch of salt
225 g (8 oz) unsalted butter
200 g (7 oz) caster sugar

100 g (3½ oz) light brown sugar
2 eggs
1 tsp vanilla essence
150 g (5 oz) gumdrops, snipped with
    floured scissors

Pre-heat the oven to 175°C (350°F / Gas mark 4). Sift the flour, bicarbonate of soda and salt together in a bowl.

Beat the butter and sugars until light and fluffy, then add the eggs and vanilla essence. Stir in the dry ingredients and gumdrops.

Drop spoonfuls onto baking sheets and bake for 12 to 15 minutes.

Transfer to wire racks to cool. When completely cool, store in an airtight container for three to four days.

Makes 2 dozen

variations

christmas tree cookies

see base recipe page 161

christmas stars
Prepare the basic cookie dough and refrigerate until firm. Roll out the dough to 6 mm (¼ in) thick and cut out star shapes using a large star-shaped cutter. Brush with egg white and sprinkle with different coloured sugar crystals. Bake, cool and decorate with sweets.

christmas angels
Prepare the basic cookie dough and refrigerate until firm. Roll out the dough to 6 mm (¼ in) thick and cut out angel shapes using a large angel-shaped cutter. Brush with egg white and sprinkle with different coloured sugar crystals. Bake, cool and decorate with sweets.

variations

cinnamon stars

see base recipe page 162

sandwich stars
Prepare the basic cookie dough. Roll the dough out to 3 mm (⅛ in) thick
and cut out the stars. Bake, cool, fill with your favourite icing and sandwich
together.

cherry stars
Prepare the basic cookie dough and add 50 g (2 oz) dried cherries to the mix
once it has formed a smooth dough.

chocolate chip cinnamon stars
Prepare the basic cookie dough and add 50 g (2 oz) plain chocolate chips
to the mix once it has formed a smooth dough.

variations

easter chocolate nest cookies

see base recipe page 165

chocolate & cherry easter nest cookies
Prepare the basic cookie dough and add 75 g (3 oz) chopped red glacé cherries to the mixture with the coconut and oats.

chocolate & raisin easter nest cookies
Prepare the basic cookie dough and add 75 g (3 oz) raisins to the mixture with the coconut and oats.

double chocolate easter nest cookies
Prepare the basic cookie dough and add 75 g (3 oz) white chocolate chips to the mixture with the coconut and oats.

variations

valentine heart cookies

see base recipe page 166

lemon valentine cookies
Prepare the basic cookie dough and add the grated zest of 1 lemon
(2 to 3 teaspoons) to the mixture.

chocolate valentine cookies
Prepare the basic cookie dough, substituting 2 tablespoons Dutch process
cocoa powder for 2 tablespoons of the plain flour.

hazelnut valentine cookies
Prepare the basic cookie dough, substituting 50 g (2 oz) toasted ground
hazelnuts for the same amount of flour.

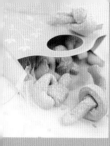

variations

lovers' knots

see base recipe page 169

orange lovers' knots
Prepare the basic cookie dough but substitute dry white wine for the rum
and orange zest for the lemon zest.

chocolate & cinnamon lovers' knots
Prepare the basic cookie dough but substitute 2 tablespoons cocoa powder
for 2 tablespoons of the flour and the 2 tablespoons caster sugar. Add
1 teaspoon ground cinnamon to the icing sugar. Toss the fried cookies in
the cinnamon sugar. Serve immediately.

lebkuchen

see base recipe page 170

crystallised lemon lebkuchen
Prepare the basic cookie dough and add 75 g (3 oz) finely chopped
crystallised lemon peel.

nutty lebkuchen
Prepare the basic cookie dough and add 75 g (3 oz) coarsely chopped
pecan nuts.

golden lebkuchen
Prepare the basic cookie dough, but substitute maple syrup for the treacle.

variations

rugelach

see base recipe page 171

lemon rugelach
Prepare the basic cookie dough and fill with a mixture of 75 g (3 oz) lemon curd and 50 g (2 oz) ground almonds.

strawberry rugelach
Prepare the basic cookie dough and fill with a mixture of 75 g (3 oz) strawberry jam and 50 g (2 oz) ground almonds.

pecan rugelach
Prepare the basic cookie dough and substitute coarsely chopped pecans for the ground almonds.

variations

giant pumpkin cookies

see base recipe page 173

spiced pumpkin cookies
Prepare the basic cookie dough and add ½ teaspoon ground cinnamon and
¼ teaspoon ground allspice to the dough. Cut out smaller cookies and bake
for 8 to 10 minutes. Decorate as for the main recipe.

raisin pumpkin cookies
Prepare the basic cookie dough and add 75 g (3 oz) raisins to the dough.

cream cheese-topped pumpkin cookies
Beat 115 g (4 oz) cream cheese with 125 g (4½ oz) icing sugar and the
grated zest of 1 lemon (2 to 3 teaspoons). Prepare the basic cookie dough
and spread the cooled cookies with the cream cheese icing and coloured
sugar crystals.

variations

layered birthday cookie

see base recipe page 174

marshmallow layered cookie
Prepare the basic cookie dough and substitute 150 g (5 oz) pink
marshmallow icing for the cream cheese and dark chocolate and
miniature marshmallows for the sweets and chocolate chips.

fresh & fruity cookie cake
Prepare the basic cookie dough, omitting the cocoa powder. Substitute
480 ml (16 fl oz) double cream for all of the filling ingredients. Whip
and sweeten the double cream with 2 teaspoons vanilla essence and
2 tablespoons icing sugar. Spread the cream on top of the cookies and
top both with fresh halved strawberries, raspberries and blueberries.

variations

witches' hats

see base recipe page 177

black cats
Prepare the basic recipe and cut out cookies using a Hallowe'en cat-shaped cutter. Decorate the cookies with black, white and silver decorations.

ghosts
Prepare the basic recipe and cut out cookies using a Hallowe'en ghost-shaped cutter. Decorate the cookies with white, silver and red decorations.

cobwebs
Prepare the basic recipe and cut out cookies using a Hallowe'en cobweb or round cutter. Decorate the cookies with white icing, pipe circles of a darker colour and drag the icing to create a cobweb effect.

variations

fortune cookies

see base recipe page 178

chocolate fortune cookies
Prepare the basic cookie dough and substitute 1 tablespoon Dutch process cocoa powder for the same amount of flour.

almond fortune cookies
Prepare the basic cookie dough and substitute almond essence for the vanilla essence.

ginger fortune cookies
Prepare the basic cookie dough and add ½ teaspoon ground ginger to the flour.

variations

gumdrop party cookies

see base recipe page 181

chocolate gumdrop cookies
Prepare the basic cookie dough and substitute 2 tablespoons Dutch
process cocoa powder for the same amount of flour.

spicy gumdrop cookies
Prepare the basic cookie dough and add 1½ teaspoons ground ginger
and ½ teaspoon ground nutmeg to the dough.

lemon gumdrop cookies
Prepare the basic cookie dough and add the grated zest of 2 lemons
(4 to 6 teaspoons).

wholesome cookies

Not all cookies and bars need to be bad for you – they can be low in fat or packed with wholesome dried fruit and healthy oats. Date bars are moist with the goodness of natural sugar and fig and walnut bites contain natural fats that are kind to the body.

muesli seed & nut bar

see variations page 215

Great for breakfast on the run, or as an energy snack at any time of day, these nutty bars are packed full of flavour.

115 g (4 oz) unsalted butter
100 g (3½ oz) demerera sugar
4 tbsp golden syrup
100 g (3½ oz) rolled oats

50 g (2 oz) muesli
2 tbsp sesame seeds
2 tbsp sunflower seeds
35 g (1¼ oz) chopped almonds

Pre-heat the oven to 175°C (375°F / Gas mark 5). Line a 18-cm- (7-in-) square baking tray with parchment. Melt the butter, sugar and golden syrup in a pan over low heat.

Blend the rolled oats in a food processor for 30 seconds. Stir the oats, muesli, seeds and almonds into the melted butter, syrup and sugar. Spread the mixture into the lined tray and level the surface with a palette knife.

Bake for 10 to 12 minutes until golden. Remove from the oven and cool in the tray for at least an hour. Remove from the tray and slice into bars.

Store in an airtight container for five to seven days.

Makes 1 dozen

sticky date bars

see variations page 216

Dates provide a quick sugar boost, so these bars are an immediate energy source.

250 g (9 oz) pitted and chopped dried dates
Grated zest (2 to 3 tsp) and juice (3 tbsp) of
    1 orange
175 g (6 oz) unsalted butter

225 g (8 oz) plain flour
2 tbsp cornflour
½ tsp baking powder
50 g (2 oz) demerera sugar

Pre-heat the oven to 175°C (375°F / Gas mark 5). Grease and line a 20 x 23-cm (8 x 9-in) tin. Put the dates, orange zest and juice in a pan and add 120 ml (4 fl oz) boiling water. Cook the dates for three to four minutes until soft, stirring all the time to make sure they don't stick. Remove from the heat. Spoon onto a plate and allow to cool.

Rub the butter into the sifted flour, cornflour and baking powder along with the sugar. Press two-thirds of the mixture into the base of the greased and lined tin.

Process the dates in a blender for 30 seconds until smooth and spread over the base in the tin. Sprinkle the remaining one-third of the mixture over the tin, pressing down lightly to give a crumbled effect. Bake for 30 to 35 minutes. Slice into bars and remove from the tin when cool.

Store in an airtight container for four to five days.

Makes 2 dozen

pumpkin cookies

see variations page 217

These moist, spicy cookies are low in fat and very simple to make.

175 g (6 oz) pumpkin puree
120 ml (4 fl oz) fat-free natural yogurt
1 tsp vanilla essence
300 g (10 oz) plain flour
1 tsp ground cinnamon
½ tsp ground ginger

½ tsp ground allspice
½ tsp ground nutmeg
½ tsp bicarbonate of soda
150 g (5 oz) raisins
150 g (5 oz) demerera sugar

Preheat the oven to 160°C (350°F / Gas mark 4). Grease two baking sheets. Mix together the pumpkin purée, yogurt and vanilla essence.

In a separate bowl sift the flour, spices and bicarbonate of soda. Add the raisins and sugar. Stir the dry ingredients into the pumpkin mixture and blend until smooth.

Drop spoonfuls onto baking sheets 5 cm (2 in) apart. Bake for 12 to 15 minutes until firm. Cool on wire racks.

When completely cool, store in an airtight container for four to five days.

Makes 3½ dozen

apricot flapjack

see variations page 218

These flapjacks aren't just a tasty treat – apricots and oats are both slow-release carbohydrates, meaning this bar will keep your hunger at bay.

350 g (12 oz) unsalted butter
5 tbsp maple syrup
300 g (10 oz) demerera sugar
450 g (1 lb) rolled oats
200 g (7 oz) chopped dried apricots

Pre-heat the oven to 175°C (375°F / Gas mark 4). Grease and line a 20 x 30-cm (8 x 12-in) tin. Melt the butter, maple syrup and sugar in a pan.

Stir in the oats and chopped apricots. Spoon the mixture into the tin and bake for 15 to 20 minutes.

Remove from the oven and allow to cool completely before cutting into squares.

Store in an airtight container for five to seven days.

Makes 2½ dozen

cherry & oatmeal cookies

see base recipe page 219

Chewy cherries give this cookie a superb texture. The demerera sugar and cinnamon give it a sweet and slightly spicy flavour.

50 g (2 oz) unsalted butter
50 g (2 oz) demerera sugar
1 egg
¼ tbsp sour cream
1 tsp vanilla essence
100 g (3½ oz) plain flour

¼ tsp bicarbonate of soda
Pinch of salt
¼ tsp ground cinnamon
½ cup oatmeal
150 g (5 oz) dried cherries

Pre-heat the oven to 175°C (350°F / Gas mark 4). In a large bowl, beat the butter and sugar together. Add the egg.

Beat in the sour cream and vanilla essence and stir in the dry ingredients and cherries.

Drop spoonfuls of the mixture onto non-stick baking sheets. Bake for 12 to 15 minutes. Cool for five minutes before removing from the sheets.

Store in an airtight container for five to seven days.

Makes 2 dozen

macadamia nut cookies

see variations page 220

Bite-sized, crisp and nutty – these cookies will disappear quicker than you think.

150 g (5 oz) macadamia nuts
2 to 3 tbsp milk
150 g (5 oz) demerera sugar
1 egg
1 tsp vanilla essence

150 g (5 oz) plain flour
¼ tsp bicarbonate of soda
¼ tsp ground nutmeg
Pinch of salt
75 g (3 oz) granulated sugar

Pre-heat the oven to 175˚C (350˚F / Gas mark 4). Put the macadamia nuts and milk into a food processor and blend for about two minutes, or until smooth. Spoon the mixture into a large bowl and add the sugar, egg and vanilla. Beat well.

Sift the flour, bicarbonate of soda, nutmeg and salt, and stir into the nut mixture to form a smooth paste.

Roll the mixture into balls and dip them into the granulated sugar. Put onto baking sheets and flatten slightly with a fork to give a criss-cross effect. Bake for 8 to 10 minutes until golden. Transfer to wire racks to cool.

When completely cool, store in an airtight container for five to seven days.

Makes 1½ dozen

muesli cookies

see variations page 221

Packed full of fruits and nuts, these cookies make a great morning snack to tide you over until lunch.

225 g (8 oz) unsalted butter
300 g (10 oz) muesli sugar
2 eggs
100 g (3½ oz) malted milk powder
300 g (10 oz) plain flour

½ tsp bicarbonate of soda
75 g (3 oz) muesli
50 g (2 oz) chopped walnuts
75 g (3 oz) raisins

Pre-heat the oven to 175°C (350°F / Gas mark 4).

Beat the butter and sugar in a bowl until fluffy. Add the eggs.

Add the dry ingredients, then stir in the dried fruit. Mix until combined.

Roll the dough into walnut-sized balls, place them on a non-stick baking sheet and press with a fork to flatten them. Bake for 15 to 18 minutes, or until golden.

Store in an airtight container for five to seven days.

Makes 3 dozen

fig & walnut bites

see variations page 222

Sweetened with unrefined maple syrup and fruit, these cookies are a wholesome antidote to a wicked sugar craving.

450 g (1 lb) walnuts
350 g (12 oz) unsalted butter
180 ml (6 fl oz) maple syrup
1 egg

1 tsp vanilla essence
225 g (8 oz) plain flour
150 g (5 oz) finely chopped figs

Pre-heat the oven to 175°C (350°F / Gas mark 4). Put the walnuts on a tray and toast in the oven for four to five minutes. Allow to cool. Beat the butter and maple syrup until light and fluffy. Add the egg and vanilla. Stir in the flour.

Put the walnuts in a food processor and blend until finely ground. Add the walnuts and figs to the dough and stir to incorporate.

Roll the dough into balls. Place 4 cm (1½ in) apart on two baking sheets and flatten slightly with a fork. Bake for 12 to 15 minutes until golden. Cool on the baking sheets before transferring to wire racks.

When completely cool, store in an airtight container for four to five days.

Makes 3 dozen

apple & prune bars

see variations page 223

Full-flavoured and fruity, these bars make ideal low-fat lunch treats.

1 egg
2 egg whites
200 g (7 oz) demerera sugar
3 tbsp safflower oil
1 tsp vanilla essence
225 g (8 oz) plain flour

1 tsp ground cinnamon
1 tsp bicarbonate of soda
Pinch of salt
150 g (5 oz) rolled oats
150 g (5 oz) chopped pitted prunes
150 g (5 oz) chopped dried apple

Pre-heat the oven to 175°C (375°F / Gas mark 5). Line a 23 x 33-cm (9 x 13-in) tin with parchment. Put the egg, egg whites and sugar in a food processor and blend until smooth. Add the oil and vanilla and process for 20 seconds to incorporate.

Add the flour, cinnamon, bicarbonate of soda and salt and process until blended. Add the oats and process for 10 seconds. Remove the mixture to a bowl and mix in the prunes and apple with a fork.

Spread the dough into the tin and level the surface. Bake for 20 to 25 minutes until a knife inserted in the centre comes out clean. Cool in the tin.

Slice into bars and store in an airtight container for four to five days.

Makes 2 dozen

sesame seed cookies

see variations page 224

Toasted sesame seeds give these cookies their wholesome touch, as well as their crunch.

150 g (5 oz) sesame seeds
75 g (3 oz) unsalted butter
150 g (5 oz) demerera sugar
1 egg

1 tsp vanilla essence
75 g (3 oz) plain flour
Pinch of baking powder
Pinch of salt

Pre-heat the oven to 175°C (375°F / Gas mark 5). Grease several baking sheets. Put the sesame seeds on a baking sheet and toast in the oven for four to five minutes or until golden.

Beat the butter and sugar until light and fluffy. Add the egg and vanilla essence.

Sift the flour, baking powder and salt and stir into the butter mixture. Stir in the sesame seeds. Drop small spoonfuls 4 cm (1½ in) apart onto baking sheets and bake for four to six minutes until golden. Cool for a few minutes on the sheets before transferring to wire racks.

Store in an airtight container for five to seven days.

Makes 3 dozen

apple-sauce cookies

see variations page 225

This reduced-sugar cookie relies on the natural sweetness of apples to save adding extra sugar. The apple-sauce also helps to make them moist.

115 g (4 oz) unsalted butter
50 g (2 oz) demerera sugar
1 egg
300 g (10 oz) plain flour
1 tsp baking powder

$\frac{1}{2}$ tsp ground cinnamon
$\frac{1}{2}$ tsp bicarbonate of soda
Pinch of salt
225 g (8 oz) unsweetened apple-sauce
2 tbsp water

Pre-heat the oven to 175°C (350°F / Gas mark 4). Beat the butter and sugar in a bowl until light and fluffy. Add the egg.

Stir in the sifted dry ingredients, apple sauce and water one at a time.

Drop teaspoonfuls onto a non-stick baking sheet and bake for 12 to 15 minutes.

Store in an airtight container for two to three days.

Makes 2½ dozen

berry oat bars

see variations page 226

Use fresh berries for an extra gooey boost; if not, frozen berries will do the trick.

115 g (4 oz) unsalted butter, melted
270 g (9½ oz) demerera sugar
200 g (7 oz) plain flour
50 g (2 oz) rolled oats
2 eggs

½ tsp baking powder
100g (3½ oz) coconut
75 g (3 oz) dried cherries
75 g (3 oz) dried blueberries
75 g (3 oz) dried strawberries

Pre-heat the oven to 175°C (375°F / Gas mark 5). Grease and line a 20 x 30-cm (8 x 12-in) tin. Mix the butter, 75 g (3 oz) sugar, 150 g (5 oz) flour and oats together. Press into the base of the tin.

In another bowl, beat the eggs and remaining sugar until light and fluffy.

Fold the remaining flour, and the baking powder, coconut and berries into the egg mixture and spread over the base. Bake for 20 to 25 minutes until golden.

Store in an airtight container for two to three days.

Makes 2 dozen

popcorn puffs

see variations page 227

Crunchy and light, these popcorn puffs are quick, simple and fun to make.

20 g (¾ oz) popcorn
3 egg whites
¼ tsp cream of tartar

100 g (3½ oz) caster sugar
½ tsp baking powder
Pinch of salt

Pre-heat the oven to 175°C (350°F / Gas mark 4). Line two baking sheets with parchment. Put the popcorn in a food processor and blend for 30 seconds. Put to one side.

Whisk the egg whites and cream of tartar. When soft peaks form, add one-third of the sugar. Whisk for one minute, then add another one-third of the sugar. Whisk for a further minute and add the rest of the sugar. Fold the popcorn, baking powder and salt into the mixture.

Drop spoonfuls onto a baking sheet and bake for 12 to 15 minutes. Transfer the parchment sheets to wire racks. Remove the popcorn puffs when cool.

Store in an airtight container for four to five days.

Makes 1½ dozen

variations

muesli seed & nut bar

see base recipe page 195

apricot seed bars
Prepare the basic cookie dough and substitute 4 tablespoons chopped
dried apricots for the chopped almonds.

honey nut bar
Prepare the basic cookie dough and substitute honey for the golden
syrup and add 50 g (2 oz) chopped pecans instead of the sunflower
and sesame seeds.

cranberry & orange breakfast bar
Prepare the basic cookie dough and substitute cranberries for the almonds.
Add the grated zest of 1 orange (2 to 3 teaspoons).

variations

sticky date bars

see base recipe page 196

apricot bars
Prepare the basic cookie dough, substituting dried apricots for the dates.

fig & cardamom bars
Prepare the basic cookie dough, adding 2 teaspoons ground cardamom seeds to the flour, and substituting figs for the dates.

blueberry & cherry bars
Prepare the basic cookie dough, substituting dried blueberries and cherries for the dates.

pumpkin cookies

see base recipe page 199

pumpkin cranberry cookies
Prepare the basic cookie dough and substitute 75 g (3 oz) dried cranberries for half of the raisins.

pumpkin apple cookies
Prepare the basic cookie dough and substitute 50 g (2 oz) chopped dried apple for half of the raisins.

pumpkin pecan cookies
Prepare the basic cookie dough and substitute 75 g (3 oz) coarsely chopped pecans for half of the raisins.

variations

apricot flapjack

see base recipe page 200

apricot & chocolate flapjack
Prepare the basic cookie dough and add 6 tablespoons Dutch process cocoa powder to the mixture when adding the oats.

peanut butter flapjack
Prepare the basic cookie dough and add 50 g (2 oz) crunchy peanut butter to the mixture when adding the oats.

ginger flapjack
Prepare the basic cookie dough and add 4 tablespoons chopped crystallised ginger to the mixture when adding the oats.

variations

cherry & oatmeal cookies

see base recipe page 201

cherry & walnut oatmeal cookies
Prepare the basic cookie dough and add 50 g (2 oz) chopped walnuts.
Decrease the cherries by half.

spiced oatmeal & raisin cookies
Prepare the basic cookie dough and substitute raisins for the cherries. Add
½ teaspoon ground ginger and ¼ teaspoon of ground allspice.

blueberry & lemon oatmeal cookies
Prepare the basic cookie dough and substitute blueberries for the cherries.
Add the grated zest of 1 lemon (2 to 3 teaspoons).

variations

macadamia nut cookies

see base recipe page 203

macadamia & cranberry cookies
Prepare the basic cookie dough and add 75 g (3 oz) dried cranberries after adding the dried ingredients.

macadamia & blueberry cookies
Prepare the basic cookie dough and add 75 g (3 oz) dried blueberries after adding the dried ingredients.

pecan & raisin cookies
Prepare the basic cookie dough and substitute pecans for the macadamia nuts. Add 75 g (3 oz) raisins after adding the dried ingredients.

variations

muesli cookies

see base recipe page 204

muesli cookies with apricot & coconut
Prepare the basic cookie dough, substituting chopped dried apricots for the raisins and 50 g (2 oz) flaked coconut for the walnuts.

spiced apple muesli cookies
Prepare the basic cookie dough, substituting 115 (4 oz) flaked coconut for the raisins, and adding 25 g (1 oz) chopped dried apple and 1 teaspoon ground cinnamon.

pecan & peach muesli cookies
Prepare the basic cookie dough, substituting chopped dried peaches for the raisins, and pecans for the walnuts.

variations

fig & walnut bites

see base recipe page 207

almond bites
Prepare the basic cookie dough and substitute almonds for the walnuts and omit the figs.

pecan & raisin bites
Prepare the basic cookie dough and substitute pecans for the walnuts and raisins for the figs.

hazelnut & cherry bites
Prepare the basic cookie dough and substitute hazelnuts for the walnuts and chopped glacé cherries for the figs.

variations

apple & prune bars

see base recipe page 208

apricot & apple bars
Prepare the basic cookie dough and substitute dried apricots for the prunes.

date & pineapple bars
Prepare the basic cookie dough and substitute dried dates and pineapple for
the prunes and apple.

coconut & cherry bars
Prepare the basic cookie dough and substitute flaked coconut for the rolled
oats and cherries for the prunes and apple.

variations

sesame seed cookies

see base recipe page 209

sesame seed & coconut cookies
Prepare the basic cookie dough and substitute 25 g (1 oz) flaked coconut for half of the sesame seeds.

sesame & cardamom cookies
Prepare the basic cookie dough and add crushed seeds from 12 cardamom pods.

sesame & ginger cookies
Prepare the basic cookie dough and add ½ teaspoon of ground ginger.

variations

apple-sauce cookies

see base recipe page 211

apple-sauce & mint cookies
Prepare the basic cookie dough and add 2 teaspoons freshly
chopped mint.

apple-sauce & pecan cookies
Prepare the basic cookie dough and add 75 g (3 oz) coarsely
chopped pecans.

apple-sauce & blueberry cookies
Prepare the basic cookie dough and add 50 g (2 oz) dried blueberries.

variations

berry oat bars

see base recipe page 212

pineapple & raisin oat bars
Prepare the basic cookie dough, substituting 150 g (5 oz) dried chopped pineapple and 75 g (3 oz) raisins for the cherries and berries.

cherry oat bars
Prepare the basic cookie dough, substituting 150 g (5 oz) dried sour cherries for the strawberries and blueberries.

pear & ginger oat bars
Prepare the basic cookie dough, substituting 100 g (3½ oz) chopped dried pears and 3 tablespoons chopped crystallised ginger for the cherries and berries.

popcorn puffs

see base recipe page 214

popcorn & fudge puffs
Prepare the basic cookie dough and add 2 tablespoons chopped
fudge pieces.

popcorn & chocolate puffs
Prepare the basic cookie dough and add 2 tablespoons plain
chocolate chips.

popcorn double deckers
Prepare and bake the basic cookie recipe. Take two cookies and sandwich
them together with low-fat cream cheese and sugar-free jam.

cookies for special diets

Just because you have a food allergy or intolerance, it doesn't mean you need to miss out on cookies and bars. Meringue cookies, macaroons, layer bars and chocolate crunchies are just a few of the recipes that are free of either gluten, dairy products, eggs or nuts.

wheat & fruit cookies

see variations page 244

Fruity, nutty, but most importantly, free of added sugar.

115 g (4 oz) unsalted butter
1 egg
Grated zest of 1 orange (2 to 3 tsp)
150 g (5 oz) wholemeal flour
1 tsp baking powder

Pinch of salt
90 g (3¼ oz) flaked coconut
150 g (5 oz) chopped dates
75 g (3 oz) ground pecans

Beat the butter and egg together. Add the orange zest and gradually stir in the wholemeal flour, baking powder and salt.

Combine the coconut, dates and pecans and stir into the cookie dough.

Divide the dough into two and roll into two logs about 6.5 cm (2½ in) in diameter. Wrap in parchment and refrigerate until firm.

Pre-heat the oven to 175°C (350°F / Gas mark 4). Slice the cookies into rounds about 6 mm (¼ in) thick. Place on baking sheets and bake for 10 to 12 minutes. Remove from the sheets and cool on wire racks.

Store in an airtight container for five to seven days.

Makes 4 dozen

macaroons

see variations page 245

A simple, wheat-free cookie that is moist and keeps well.

115 g (4 oz) ground almonds
250 g (9 oz) caster sugar
1 tbsp ground rice
2 egg whites

Preheat the oven to 175°C (350°F / Gas mark 4). Line baking sheets with rice paper. Mix all the ingredients to a smooth paste.

Pipe small rounds of mixture using a 1-cm (½-in) plain nozzle.

Bake for 8 to 10 minutes until golden. Cool on baking sheets and peel off the rice paper to remove.

When completely cool, store in an airtight container for five to seven days.

Makes 2 dozen

almond cookies

see variations page 246

Whether you follow a wheat-free diet or not, you'll love these buttery, crunchy, wheat-free cookies.

115 g (4 oz) unsalted butter
100 g (3½ oz) light brown sugar
1 egg

100 g (3½ oz) rice flour
50 g (2 oz) crisped rice cereal
2 tbsp chopped almonds

Pre-heat the oven to 175°C (350°F / Gas mark 4). Beat the butter and sugar together until soft. Add the egg.

Fold in the rice flour, cereal and almonds.

Roll the dough into balls, place on a large, non-stick baking sheet and press them with a fork to flatten. Bake for 12 to 15 minutes.

Store in an airtight container for three to four days.

Makes 1½ dozen

banana cookies

see variations page 247

Big on flavour and very easy to make, these cookies require no added sugar to sweeten them, relying on the natural fruit sugars in the bananas and dates. Made without wheat flour, they are perfect for anyone who wants a healthy, wheat-free snack.

3 ripe bananas
150 g (5 oz) pitted dates
200 g (7 oz) rolled oats

Pre-heat the oven to 175°C (350°F / Gas mark 4).

Mash the bananas and chop the dates fine. Mix all the ingredients in a bowl together and put to one side for 15 minutes.

Drop teaspoonfuls onto a non-stick baking sheet and bake for 20 minutes.

Store in an airtight container and eat within 24 hours.

Makes 2½ dozen

coconut wedges

see variations page 248

Dairy-free and sweetened with maple syrup, this coconut oat cookie is a wholesome alternative to mass-produced snack bars.

190 g (9½ oz) plain flour
½ tsp baking powder
½ tsp bicarbonate of soda
½ tsp ground cinnamon
¼ tsp ground nutmeg
135 g (4¾ oz) dessicated coconut

50 g (2 oz) rolled oats
115 g (4 oz) coarsely chopped pecans
120 ml (4 fl oz) safflower oil
180 ml (6 fl oz) maple syrup
2 eggs
2 tsp vanilla essence

Pre-heat the oven to 175°C (350°F / Gas mark 4). Grease and line a 23 x 33-cm (9 x 13-in) tin with parchment.

Sift the flour, baking powder, bicarbonate of soda and spices together in a bowl and stir in the coconut, oats and pecans.

Beat the oil and maple syrup together. Add the eggs and vanilla essence.

Stir the dry ingredients into the oil and egg mixture. Spread the mixture into the tin. Bake for 12 to 15 minutes. Cut into wedges and transfer to a wire rack to cool. Store in an airtight container for four to five days.

Makes 2 dozen

dairy-free shortbread

see variations page 249

Crisp, crumbly and dairy-free, this shortbread is too tasty to resist!

175 g (6 oz) margarine
100 g (3½ oz) caster sugar
2 tsp vanilla essence

200 g (7oz) plain flour
¼ tsp salt
2 tsp granulated sugar

Line a 23-cm (9-in) round tin with foil.

Cut the margarine into chunks and gently melt it in a saucepan over a low heat. Remove from the heat and stir in the caster sugar and vanilla essence.

Sift the flour and salt together and stir into the sugar mixture. Spread the mixture evenly into the pan and refrigerate for two hours, or until firm.

Pre-heat the oven to 150°C (300°F / Gas mark 2). Bake for 55 to 60 minutes. Remove from the oven and sprinkle with granulated sugar. Cut into wedges and cool in the tin.

Store in an airtight container for five to seven days.

Makes 1 dozen

layer bars

see variations page 250

A gluten-free sweet treat that even kids will love.

75 g (3 oz) unsalted butter
200 g (7 oz) gluten-free cookie crumbs
150 g (5 oz) plain chocolate chips
150 g (5 oz) white chocolate chips

150 g (5 oz) coarsely chopped pecans
90 g (3¼ oz) flaked coconut
250 ml (8 fl oz) condensed milk

Pre-heat the oven to 160°C (325°F / Gas mark 3). Line a 20-cm- (8-in-) square tin with parchment.

Melt the butter in a saucepan, remove from the heat and stir in the cookie crumbs. Press into the tin.

Sprinkle over the chocolate chips, pecans and coconut. Pour over the condensed milk.

Bake for 30 to 35 minutes. Cool in the tin for at least an hour and cut into bars.

Store in an airtight container for three to four days.

Makes 2½ dozen

berry meringue cookies

see variations page 251

Meringue cookies that can be dressed up as a fancy dessert – simply by sandwiching two together with fruit jam or whipped cream.

3 egg whites
¼ tsp cream of tartar
100 g (3½ oz) caster sugar
1 tbsp cornflour

1 tsp white wine vinegar
50 g (2 oz) finely chopped dried blueberries
50 g (2 oz) finely chopped dried cherries

Pre-heat the oven to 140°C (275°F / Gas mark 1). Line two baking sheets with parchment. Whisk the egg whites and cream of tartar together. When soft peaks form, add one-third of the sugar. Whisk for another minute and add another third of the sugar. Whisk for a further minute and add the remaining sugar.

Mix the cornflour with the vinegar and stir into the meringue. Stir in the dried berries.

Drop spoonfuls onto a baking sheet and flatten with the back of the spoon. Bake for 25 to 30 minutes, turn off the oven and leave inside for an hour. Transfer the parchment sheets to wire racks. Remove when cool.

Store in an airtight container for two to three days.

Makes 1½ dozen

meringue nut cookies

see variations page 252

Nutty little mouthfuls that are light enough to eat at any time of day.

3 egg whites
¼ tsp cream of tartar
100 g (3½ oz) caster sugar
4 tbsp toasted ground hazelnuts

150 g (5 oz) coarsely chopped
   toasted hazelnuts
Pinch of salt

Pre-heat the oven to 140°C (275°F / Gas mark 1). Line two baking sheets with parchment.

Whisk the egg whites and cream of tartar together. When soft peaks form, add one-third of the sugar. Whisk for a further minute, then add another third of the sugar. Whisk for another minute and add the remaining sugar.

Fold the hazelnuts and salt into the meringue.

Drop spoonfuls onto a baking sheet and bake for 25 to 30 minutes. Turn off the oven and leave inside for an hour. Transfer the parchment sheets to wire racks. Remove when cool.

Store in an airtight container for four to five days.

Makes 2 dozen

55

dark chocolate crunchies

see variations page 253

These are everyone's favourite refrigerator cookie – and especially easy for kids to make.

200 g (7 oz) dark chocolate
50 g (2 oz) unsalted butter
5 tbsp golden syrup
100 g (3½ oz) crisped rice cereal

Line two baking sheets with parchment.

Melt the chocolate and butter together in a heatproof bowl over a saucepan of simmering water or in the microwave.

Stir in the golden syrup and crisped rice cereal. Drop spoonfuls of the mixture onto the baking sheets and refrigerate for about 45 minutes, until set.

Store in an airtight container in the fridge for five to seven days.

Makes 2 dozen

variations

wheat & fruit cookies

see base recipe page 229

date & walnut cookies
Prepare the basic cookie dough and substitute walnuts for the pecans.

fig & raisin cookies
Prepare the basic cookie dough and substitute 75 g (3 oz) raisins and 75 g (3 oz) chopped figs for the dates.

variations

macaroons

see base recipe page 231

pistachio macaroons
Prepare the basic cookie dough and substitute ground pistachios for half the ground almonds. Top each piped macaroon with a pistachio.

walnut macaroons
Prepare the basic cookie dough and substitute ground walnuts for half the ground almonds. Top each piped macaroon with a walnut half.

hazelnut macaroons
Prepare the basic cookie dough and substitute ground hazelnuts for half the ground almonds. Top each piped macaroon with a hazelnut.

variations

almond cookies

see base recipe page 232

almond & cherry cookies
Prepare the basic cookie dough and add 50 g (2 oz) dried cherries.

pine nut & lemon cookies
Prepare the basic cookie dough, substituting pine nuts for the almonds.

almond & cranberry cookies
Prepare the basic cookie dough and add 50 g (2 oz) dried cranberries.

variations

banana cookies

see base recipe page 233

banana & rum cookies
Prepare the basic cookie dough and add 2 tablespoons dark rum.

spiced banana cookies
Prepare the basic cookie dough, and add ½ teaspoon ground cinnamon
and ¼ teaspoon ground ginger.

banana & coconut cookies
Prepare the basic cookie dough, substituting flaked coconut for
50 g (2 oz) of the rolled oats.

variations

coconut wedges

see base recipe page 234

pineapple coconut wedges
Prepare the basic cookie dough and substitute 75 g (3 oz) chopped dried pineapple for the pecans.

cherry coconut wedges
Prepare the basic cookie dough and substitute 75 g (3 oz) dried cherries for the pecans.

apricot coconut wedges
Prepare the basic cookie dough and substitute 75 g (3 oz) chopped dried apricots for the pecans.

dairy-free shortbread

see base recipe page 236

brown sugar shortbread
Prepare the basic cookie dough and substitute unrefined dark brown sugar
for half of the caster sugar.

spiced pecan shortbread
Prepare the basic cookie dough, decreasing the flour to 190 g (6½ oz).
Process 75 g (3 oz) whole toasted pecans until they are finely ground,
and then add the nuts to the flour with ½ teaspoon ground cinnamon
and ¼ teaspoon ground nutmeg.

cherry shortbread
Prepare the basic cookie dough, and add 150 g (5 oz) chopped red glacé
cherries to the mixture with the flour.

variations

layer bars

see base recipe page 237

butterscotch layer bars
Prepare the basic cookie dough and substitute butterscotch chips for the white chocolate chips.

peanut layer bars
Prepare the basic cookie dough and substitute peanuts for the pecans.

raisin layer bars
Prepare the basic cookie dough and substitute raisins for the white chocolate chips.

berry meringue cookies

see base recipe page 239

fresh berry meringues
Prepare the basic cookie dough and substitute 75 g (3 oz) fresh blueberries
for the dried berries. You will need to eat these meringues on the day they
are made.

cranberry meringues
Prepare the basic cookie dough and substitute cranberries and the grated
zest of one orange (1 to 2 teaspoons) for the blueberries and cherries.

blueberry & lemon meringues
Prepare the basic cookie dough, but substitute more dried blueberries for
the dried cherries. Add the grated zest of one lemon (1 to 2 teaspoons).

variations

meringue nut cookies

see base recipe page 240

macadamia meringue nut cookies
Prepare the basic cookie dough and substitute macadamia nuts for the hazelnuts.

pecan & cinnamon meringue nut cookies
Prepare the basic cookie dough and substitute pecans for the hazelnuts. Add ½ teaspoon ground cinnamon to the sugar.

brazil nut meringue cookies
Prepare the basic cookie dough and substitute brazil nuts for the hazelnuts. Replace half the caster sugar with demerera sugar.

variations

dark chocolate crunchies

see base recipe page 243

chocolate raisin crunchies
Prepare the basic cookie dough and add 75 g (3 oz) raisins to the mixture.

chocolate chip & pecan crunchies
Prepare the basic cookie dough and add 75 g (3 oz) white chocolate chips
and ½ cup (3 oz) coarsely chopped pecans to the mixture.

chocolate cherry crunchies
Prepare the basic cookie dough and add 75 g (3 oz) chopped red glacé
cherries to the mixture.

cookie bars

Rather than shaping into individual cookies, these classic cookies are baked in a tray and then sliced into wedges, squares or fingers. Brownies, fruit and nut slices, millionaire's shortbread and turtle bars – cookie bars have become so popular they deserve a chapter of their own.

lemon bars

see variations page 273

These sharp-tasting little bars are sure to become a firm favourite with the family.

for the crust

115 g (4 oz) unsalted butter
50 g (2 oz) caster sugar
1 tsp vanilla essence
150 g (5 oz) plain flour
Pinch of salt

for the topping

50 g (2 oz) caster sugar
2 tbsp plain flour
2 eggs
150 g (5 oz) lemon curd
5 tbsp fresh lemon juice
2 tbsp icing sugar to dust

Pre-heat the oven to 175°C (350°F / Gas mark 4). Line a 20-cm- (8-in-) square tin with foil. Cut the butter into chunks and melt in a saucepan over a gentle heat. Remove from the heat and stir in the sugar and vanilla essence. Then stir in the sifted flour and salt. Press the dough into the bottom of the tin. Bake for 30 minutes until the crust is golden. Remove from the oven and reduce the temperature to 150°C (300°F / Gas mark 2).

While the crust is baking, stir together the sugar and flour for the topping in a large bowl. Whisk in the eggs. Stir in the lemon curd and lemon juice. When the crust is cooked, pour the filling over the base and bake for 20 minutes or until lightly set. Cool in the tin then transfer the foil to a chopping board. Cut into squares and store in an airtight container for two to three days. Before serving, dust with icing sugar.

Makes 2½ dozen

brownies

see variations page 274

Everyone loves brownies and everyone has a favourite recipe. This is mine, adapted from a recipe given to me by my friend, a pastry chef, who used to make brownies in Joe Allen Restaurant in London, England.

115 g (4 oz) unsalted butter
4 oz bitter chocolate
4 oz dark chocolate
200 g (7 oz) demerera sugar
Pinch of salt

1 tsp vanilla essence
2 eggs
40 g (1½ oz) plain flour
150 g (5 oz) coarsely chopped pecans

Pre-heat the oven to 160°C (325°F / Gas mark 3). Line the base and sides of a 20-cm- (8-in-) square tin with parchment.

Melt the butter and chocolate in a heatproof bowl over a saucepan of simmering water or in the microwave on a low heat. Once melted, stir to blend the butter and chocolate together, then add the sugar, salt and vanilla. Beat in the eggs one at a time, then beat in the flour and half the pecans. When the batter is smooth, pour into the tin, sprinkle over the remaining pecans and bake for 35 to 40 minutes.

Cool in the tin for at least 20 minutes. Lift the parchment and transfer the brownies to a chopping board. Cut into squares and store in an airtight container for three to four days.

Makes 2½ dozen

nut brittle squares

see variations page 275

Crunchy fruit and nut bites to accompany the froth on your morning cappuccino.

for the crust

115 g (4 oz) unsalted butter
200 g (7 oz) plain flour
¼ tsp salt
50 g (2 oz) caster sugar
1 egg

for the topping

300 g (10 oz) unsalted butter
115 g (4 oz) clear honey
312 g (10½ oz) caster sugar
5 tbsp double cream
1 cup (3½ oz) coarsely chopped crystallised fruit
1 cup (3½ oz) coarsely chopped hazelnuts
1 cup (3½ oz) coarsely chopped walnuts

Pre-heat the oven to 175°C (350°F / Gas mark 4). Line a 23 x 33-cm (9 x 13-in) tin with parchment. Cut the butter into chunks and put into the food processor with the flour, salt and sugar. Process until the mixture resembles breadcrumbs, then add the egg and process until the mixture comes together. Press into the base of the tin. Bake for 15 to 20 minutes until golden. Put the butter, honey and sugar in a heavy saucepan and cook over a moderate heat for 15 to 20 minutes, stirring frequently. Remove from the heat and stir in the cream, fruit and nuts. Pour onto the crust, level the surface, put the tin on a baking sheet and bake for 15 to 20 minutes. Remove from the oven and allow to cool before cutting into squares.

Store in an airtight container for five to seven days.

Makes 2½ dozen

toffee bars

see variations page 276

Buttery shortbread and lashings of chocolate studded with nuts and fudge pieces make these a favourite with the kids.

for the crust

115 g (4 oz) unsalted butter
100 g (3½ oz) light brown sugar
1 tsp vanilla essence
150 g (5 oz) plain flour
Pinch of salt

for the topping

175 g (6 oz) plain chocolate, chopped into
    small pieces
75 g (2 oz) chopped fudge pieces
75 g (2 oz) chopped toasted almonds

Pre-heat the oven to 175°C (350°F / Gas mark 4). Line the base and sides of a 20-cm- (8-in-) square tin with foil.

Cut the butter into chunks and melt in a saucepan over a gentle heat. Remove from the heat and stir in the sugar and vanilla essence. Then stir in the sifted flour and salt. Press the dough into the bottom of the tin.

Bake for 20 to 25 minutes until golden. Remove from the oven and sprinkle with chocolate, fudge pieces and almonds and return to the oven for two to three minutes to melt the chocolate. Allow to cool in the tin, then lift the foil and transfer to a chopping board. Cut into bars. Store in an airtight container for five to seven days.

Makes 2½ dozen

honey nut squares

see variations page 277

These chewy honey squares are packed full of crunchy nuts surrounded by soft toffee.

for the crust

115 g (4 oz) unsalted butter
200 g (7 oz) plain flour
¼ tsp salt
50 g (2 oz) caster sugar
1 egg

for the topping

225 g (8 oz) lightly toasted macadamia nuts
150 g (5 oz) caster sugar
50 g (2 oz) honey
115 g (4 oz) unsalted butter
150 ml (5 fl oz) double cream

Preheat the oven to 175°C (350°F / Gas mark 4). Line a 23 x 33-cm (9 x 13-in) tin with parchment. Put the butter in a food processor with the flour, salt and sugar. Process until the mixture resembles breadcrumbs, then add the egg and process until it comes together. Press into the base of the tin. Bake for 15 to 20 minutes until golden.

Process the macadamia nuts in a food processor for 30 seconds. Put the sugar, honey, butter and cream into a heavy saucepan and using a sugar thermometer, cook to soft ball stage 118°C (240°F). Put the nuts on a baking sheet and warm in the oven for a few minutes. Remove the thermometer and place it in a jug of boiling water. Take the pan off the heat and quickly stir in the warmed nuts. Pour the mixture onto the crust and bake for five minutes. Remove from the oven and allow to set for about two hours. Cut into squares and store in an airtight container for five to seven days.

Makes 2 dozen

turtle bars

see variations page 278

If you have not tried turtle bars – you need to! This wonderful combination of American flavours is divine – chewy caramel, pecans and chocolate on a shortbread base.

for the crust

175 g (6 oz) unsalted butter
50 g (2 oz) caster sugar
1 tsp vanilla essence
300 g (10 oz) plain flour
Pinch of salt
200 g (7 oz) pecan halves

for the topping

115 g (4 oz) unsalted butter
150 g (5 oz) light brown sugar
150 g (5 oz) plain chocolate chips

Pre-heat the oven to 175°C (350°F / Gas mark 4). Line a 23 x 33-cm (9 x 13-in) tin with foil. Cut the butter into chunks and melt in a saucepan over a gentle heat. Remove from the heat and stir in the sugar and vanilla. Stir in the sifted flour and salt. Press the dough into the bottom of the tin. Bake for 10 minutes then scatter over the pecans and bake for 10 minutes more until the crust is golden. Remove from the oven.

Melt the butter and stir in the sugar. Bring the mixture to the boil and boil for one minute. Pour the hot butter mixture over the crust. Bake for 10 minutes, then remove from the oven and sprinkle over the chocolate chips. Cool in the tin. Lift the foil and transfer to a chopping board. Cut into bars. Store in an airtight container for five to seven days.

Makes 2 dozen

chewy almond cherry bars

see variations page 279

Super little snack bars that are light, tasty and not too sweet.

150 g (5 oz) whole almonds
100 g (3½ oz) plain flour
½ tsp baking powder
Pinch of salt

115 g (4 oz) unsalted butter
150 g (5 oz) light brown sugar
1 egg
75 g (3 oz) dried cherries

Pre-heat the oven to 175°C (350°F / Gas mark 4). Line the base and sides of a 20-cm- (8-in-) square tin with parchment.

Put the almonds in a food processor and process until they are finely ground. Then add the flour, baking powder and salt and process to mix.

Cut the butter into chunks and melt in a saucepan over a gentle heat. Remove from the heat and stir in the sugar and egg. Then stir in the dry ingredients and cherries. Spread the mixture into the tin and bake for 20 to 25 minutes until golden. Cool in the tin. Lift the parchment and transfer to a chopping board. Cut into bars.

Store in an airtight container for five to seven days.

Makes 2½ dozen

fruit & nut slices

see variations page 280

These tasty bars make an irresistible mid-morning snack.

40 g (1½ oz) plain flour
Pinch of baking powder
Pinch of bicarbonate of soda
Pinch of salt
50 g (2 oz) light brown sugar

200 g (7 oz) pecan pieces
225 g (8 oz) stoned and chopped dates
150 g (5 oz) coarsely chopped dried apricots
1 egg
1 tsp vanilla essence

Pre-heat the oven to 175°C (350°F / Gas mark 4). Line the base and sides of a 20-cm- (8-in-) square tin with parchment.

Sift the flour, baking powder, bicarbonate of soda and salt together in a bowl. Add the sugar and fruits and coat them in the flour. In a separate bowl, beat the egg and vanilla until pale and thick, then add to the fruit and flour mix. Mix with your hands until all the fruit is evenly coated in the mixture. Spread the mixture into the tin and bake for 35 to 40 minutes until golden brown. Lift the parchment and transfer to a chopping board. Cut into slices.

Store in an airtight container for five to seven days.

Makes 2½ dozen

cream cheese cookie slices

see variations page 281

Chocolate and cream cheese combine to great effect in these cookie slices.

175 g (6 oz) unsalted butter
200 g (7 oz) dark chocolate
400 g (14 oz) caster sugar
4 eggs

2 tsp vanilla essence
300 g (10 oz) plain flour
225 g (8 oz) cream cheese
150 g (5 oz) coarsely chopped plain chocolate

Pre-heat the oven to 175°C (350°F / Gas mark 4). Line a 23 x 33-cm (9 x 13-in) tin with parchment. Melt the butter and dark chocolate in a heatproof bowl over a saucepan of simmering water or in the microwave on low. Once melted, stir to blend the butter and chocolate together, then add 300 g (10 oz) of sugar, the eggs and the vanilla essence. Stir in the flour and spread the mixture in the tin.

Beat the cream cheese and remaining sugar and stir in the plain chocolate chunks. Drop spoonfuls over the chocolate mixture and swirl the two together to give a marbled effect. Bake for 30 to 35 minutes until lightly set. Cool completely in the tin. Lift the parchment and transfer to a chopping board. Cut into bars.

Store in an airtight container and refrigerate for three to four days.

Makes 2 dozen

blondies

see variations page 282

As their name suggests, blondies are golden in colour. Light brown sugar gives the best result. This version, packed full of nuts and chocolate chips, is fantastic.

150 g (5 oz) plain flour
¾ tsp baking powder
Pinch of salt
115 g (4 oz) unsalted butter
200 g (5 oz) light brown sugar

1 egg
1 tsp vanilla essence
115 g (4 oz) coarsely chopped walnuts
115 g (4 oz) plain chocolate chips

Pre-heat the oven to 175°C (350°F / Gas mark 4). Line the base and sides of a 20-cm- (8-in-) square tin with parchment.

Sift the flour, baking powder and salt together in a bowl. Cut the butter into chunks and melt in a saucepan over a gentle heat. Remove from the heat and stir in the brown sugar. Beat in the egg and vanilla, then stir in the flour mixture, walnuts and chocolate chips. Spread the mixture in the tin and bake for 20 to 25 minutes until golden. Remove from the oven and allow to cool in the tin. Lift the parchment and transfer the blondies to a chopping board.

Cut into squares and store in an airtight container for two to three days.

Makes 2 dozen

tropical bars

see variations page 283

Eating these tangy, fruity bars is a full-blown Calypso experience you must not miss out on – once tasted, never forgotten.

150 g (5 oz) unsalted butter	50 g (2 oz) chopped dried mango
225 g (8 oz) peanut butter	50 g (2 oz) chopped dried pineapple
100 g (3½ oz) light brown sugar	1 tbsp flaked coconut
75 g (3 oz) chopped dates	65 g (2½ oz) crisped rice cereal

Line a 20-cm- (8-in-) square tin with parchment.

Cut the butter into chunks and melt in a saucepan over a gentle heat. Stir in the peanut butter and then the sugar and stir to combine.

Remove from the heat and add the dates, dried mango and pineapple. Stir in the coconut and rice cereal. Press the mixture into the tin and refrigerate until firm. Remove from the tin and cut into bars.

Store in an airtight container in the fridge for five to seven days.

Makes 2½ dozen

white chocolate fudge bars

see variations page 284

Wonderfully moist with a touch of vanilla, these white chocolate fudge bars are a change from the usual chocolate bars.

225 g (8 oz) plain flour
½ tsp bicarbonate of soda
115 g (4 oz) unsalted butter
75 g (3 oz) white chocolate
2 eggs

400 g (14 oz) caster sugar
2 tsp vanilla essence
75 g (3 oz) chopped toasted hazelnuts
75 g (3 oz) white chocolate chips

Pre-heat the oven to 175°C (350°F / Gas mark 4). Line a 23 x 33-cm- (9 x 13-in-) deep tin with parchment. Sift the flour and bicarbonate of soda together in a bowl. Melt the butter and white chocolate in a heatproof bowl over a saucepan of simmering water, or in the microwave on a low heat. In a separate bowl, beat the eggs until foamy, then beat in the sugar until well blended. Stir in the melted chocolate, butter and vanilla essence.

Add the dry ingredients and spoon into the tin. Level the surface and sprinkle with the chocolate chips. Place the tin on a baking sheet and bake for 25 to 30 minutes. Remove from the oven, allow to cool in the tin for 10 minutes, then invert onto parchment on a wire tray and cool for 30 minutes. Invert onto a chopping board and cut into bars.

When completely cool, store in an airtight container for five to seven days.

Makes 2 dozen

millionaire's shortbread

see variations page 285

Millionaire's shortbread is appropriately named, given that it is rich and extravagant!

200 g (7 oz) plain flour
50 g (2 oz) icing sugar
350 g (12 oz) unsalted butter
5 tbsp golden syrup

One 400-g (14-oz) can condensed milk
1 tsp vanilla essence
200 g (7 oz) plain chocolate
1 tbsp safflower oil

Pre-heat the oven to 175°C (350°F / Gas mark 4). Line the base of a 23 x 33-cm (9 x 13-in) tin with foil. Sift the flour and icing sugar together in a bowl and then rub in 225 g (8 oz) butter until the mixture starts to come together. Press the dough into the base of the tin. Bake for 15 to 20 minutes until golden.

For the caramel, melt the remaining butter in the microwave and then stir in the golden syrup and condensed milk. Microwave on high for eight to nine minutes, stirring every one to two minutes. Stir in the vanilla and spread over the warm shortbread. Refrigerate for about two hours until firm. Melt the chocolate in a heatproof bowl over a saucepan of simmering water or in the microwave on a low heat, then stir in the safflower oil. Spread over the caramel and refrigerate for 15 minutes, then cut into squares.

When completely cool, store in an airtight container for five to seven days.

Makes 2½ dozen

variations

lemon bars

see base recipe page 255

hazelnut-crusted lemon bars
Prepare the basic cookie dough, putting the sugar, salt and all but
3 tablespoons of the flour in a food processor with 50 g (2 oz) toasted
skinned hazelnuts. Grind the mixture to a fine powder, then add the melted
butter. Press into the tin and bake. Prepare the topping in the base recipe.

apricot & lemon bars
Prepare the basic cookie dough substituting apricot jam for the lemon curd.

lemon & lime bars
Prepare the basic cookie dough, substituting lime juice for the lemon juice.

variations

brownies

see base recipe page 257

chocolate chip brownies
Prepare the basic cookie dough and substitute 75 g (3 oz) plain chocolate chips for the pecans.

cream cheese brownies
Prepare the basic cookie dough, then put a third of the mixture into a separate bowl. Add 115 g (4 oz) cream cheese and mix to incorporate. Pour the chocolate brownie mixture into the tin and swirl through the cream cheese mixture to give a marbled effect.

mocha brownies
Prepare the basic cookie dough and add 75 g (3 oz) plain chocolate chips and 2 tablespoons strong instant coffee powder to the mixture.

variations

nut brittle squares

see base recipe page 258

cherry nut brittle squares
Prepare the basic cookie dough, and substitute 50 g (2 oz) dried cherries
and 50 g (2 oz) chopped glacé cherries for the crystallised fruit.

pecan & chocolate nut brittle squares
Prepare the basic cookie dough, and substitute pecans for the walnuts and
50 g (2 oz) chopped glacé cherries and 50 g (2 oz) plain chocolate chips for
the crystallised fruit.

almond & ginger nut brittle squares
Prepare the basic cookie dough, and substitute flaked almonds for the
walnuts, and 50 g (2 oz) chopped crystallised ginger for the crystallised fruit.

variations

toffee bars

see base recipe page 259

cherry toffee bars
Prepare the basic cookie dough and substitute chopped red glacé cherries for the fudge pieces.

hazelnut toffee bars
Prepare the basic cookie dough and substitute skinned chopped toasted hazelnuts for the almonds.

white chocolate chip toffee bars
Prepare the basic cookie dough and add 50 g (2 oz) white chocolate chips to the topping.

variations

honey nut squares

see base recipe page 260

pecan honey nut squares
Prepare the basic cookie dough, and substitute pecans for the macadamia
nuts. As pecans are softer than macadamias, process them for only about
20 seconds in the food processor.

walnut, honey & cherry squares
Prepare the basic cookie dough, substituting walnuts for the macadamia
nuts and add 75 g (3 oz) chopped red glacé cherries with the nuts.

almond & ginger honey nut squares
Prepare the basic cookie dough, substituting whole skinned almonds for
the macadamia nuts, and add 2 tablespoons chopped crystallised ginger
with the nuts.

variations

turtle bars

see base recipe page 263

double chocolate nut turtle bars
Prepare the basic cookie dough, substituting skinned hazelnuts for half
the pecans and white chocolate chips for half the plain chocolate.

fudge turtle bars
Prepare the basic cookie dough and add 75 g (3 oz) chopped fudge
pieces to the hot topping before the chocolate chips.

marshmallow turtle bars
Prepare the basic cookie dough and add 50 g (2 oz) miniature marshmallows
to the hot topping before the chocolate chips.

chewy almond cherry bars

see base recipe page 264

almond & date bars
Prepare the basic cookie dough and substitute 75 g (3 oz) chopped dates for the cherries.

cranberry, orange & almond bars
Prepare the basic cookie dough and substitute 75 g (3 oz) dried cranberries for the cherries, and add the grated zest of 1 orange (2 to 3 teaspoons).

hazelnut pear bars
Prepare the basic cookie dough and substitute hazelnuts for the almonds and chopped dried pear for the cherries.

variations

fruit & nut slices

see base recipe page 265

blueberry & walnut slices
Prepare the basic cookie dough and substitute walnuts for the pecans and dried blueberries for the dates.

pear & almond slices
Prepare the basic cookie dough and substitute coarsely chopped almonds for the pecans and chopped dried pears for the apricots.

pineapple & apricot slices
Prepare the basic cookie dough and substitute 75 g (3 oz) chopped dried pineapple for 75 g (3 oz) of the dates.

variations

cream cheese cookie slices

see base recipe page 266

chocolate-orange cream cheese cookie slices
Prepare the basic cookie dough and add the grated zest of 1 orange
(2 to 3 teaspoons) to the chocolate mixture.

fudge-nut cream cheese cookie slices
Prepare the basic cookie dough and add 75 g (3 oz) coarsely chopped pecans
to the chocolate mixture and 75 g (3 oz) chopped fudge pieces to the cream
cheese mixture.

mocha cream cheese cookie slices
Prepare the basic cookie dough and add 2 tablespoons instant coffee powder
to the cream cheese mixture before swirling it in the chocolate mixture.

variations

blondies

see base recipe page 268

butterscotch blondies
Prepare the basic cookie dough and substitute 50 g (2 oz) butterscotch chips for 50 g (2 oz) walnuts.

pecan & white chocolate chip blondies
Prepare the basic cookie dough and substitute pecans for the walnuts and white chocolate chips for the plain chocolate chips.

double chocolate chip blondies
Prepare the basic cookie dough and substitute 50 g (2 oz) white chocolate chips for half the walnuts.

variations

tropical bars

see base recipe page 269

date & cherry bars
Prepare the basic cookie dough and substitute chopped red glacé cherries for the dried mango and pineapple.

chocolate & coconut bars
Prepare the basic cookie dough and substitute 75 g (3 oz) plain chocolate chips for the dried mango and pineapple.

ginger tropical bars
Prepare the basic cookie dough and add 2 tablespoons chopped crystallised ginger.

variations

white chocolate fudge bars

see base recipe page 271

white chocolate butterscotch bars
Prepare the basic cookie dough and substitute light brown sugar for
the caster sugar and butterscotch chips for the white chocolate chips.

double chocolate fudge bars
Prepare the basic cookie dough and substitute dark chocolate for
the white chocolate.

chocolate cherry fudge bars
Prepare the basic cookie dough and substitute dark chocolate for
the white chocolate, and add 75 g (3 oz) chopped red glacé cherries.

millionaire's shortbread

see base recipe page 272

chocolate chip millionaire's shortbread
Prepare the basic cookie dough and sprinkle 50 g (2 oz) dark chocolate chips over the shortbread base before spreading the caramel on top.

chocolate orange millionaire's shortbread
Prepare the basic cookie dough, adding the grated zest of 1 orange (2 to 3 teaspoons) to the chocolate before spreading it over the firm caramel.

nut-crusted millionaire's shortbread
Prepare the basic cookie dough but substitute 40 g (1½ oz) toasted ground hazelnuts for 40 g (1½ oz) of the flour.

dessert cookies

Delicate wafer-thin cookies such as lacy wafers and brandy snaps can transform a simple bowl of ice cream into a sophisticated dessert. This chapter is dedicated to your dinner guests, with ideas of what to serve with coffee and wine and how to impress with home-made macaroons and amaretti.

langue de chat

see variations page 310

Langue de chat, or 'cats' tongue', is a wafer-thin delicate biscuit that can be served with ice cream sundaes or individual mousse desserts.

50 g (2 oz) unsalted butter
50 g (2 oz) icing sugar, sifted
2 egg whites
65 g (2½ oz) plain flour, sifted

Pre-heat the oven to 200°C (400°F / Gas mark 6). Grease two baking sheets.

Beat the butter and sugar together until light and fluffy. Add the egg whites and mix to incorporate. Stir in the sifted flour.

Pipe the mixture using a piping bag and a 6-mm (¼-in) plain nozzle, making 4-cm (1½-in) lengths 4 cm (1½ in) apart. Bake for four to five minutes until golden. Remove from the oven and transfer to a wire rack.

When cool, store in an airtight container for five to seven days.

Makes 3 dozen

french macaroons

see variations page 311

These light macaroons can be found throughout the pâtisseries of Paris.

375 g (13 oz) icing sugar
250 g (9 oz) ground almonds
7 egg whites

A couple of drops pink food colouring
¼ tsp cream of tartar
75 g (3 oz) strawberry jam

Preheat the oven to 200°C (400°F / Gas mark 6). Line two baking sheets with parchment. Sift the icing sugar and mix 225 g (8 oz) together with the almonds. Beat in three of the egg whites and enough food colouring to turn the mixture light pink. Beat the remaining four egg whites with the cream of tartar until soft peaks form. Add one-third of the remaining sugar. Beat for one to two minutes until the egg whites are stiff and add another third of the sugar. Beat for one minute and add the remaining sugar. Beat until the meringue is glossy. Add a quarter of the meringue to the dry ingredients and blend – do not try to fold in all the meringue at this stage. Add another quarter of the meringue and lift the mixture through with a balloon whisk. Add the remaining meringue in the same way.

Pipe the mixture using a piping bag and 1-cm (½-in) nozzle, making 2.5-cm (1-in) bulbs, 2.5 cm (1 in) apart on the baking sheets. Bake for five to six minutes. Allow to cool and remove from the parchment. Spread the bases of half the macaroons with strawberry jam and sandwich with the remaining halves. Store in an airtight container for five to seven days.

Makes 2 dozen

brandy snaps

see variations page 312

Lacy in appearance, these spicy cookies are divine either filled with cream or simply served plain with ice cream.

115 g (4 oz) unsalted butter
115 g (4 oz) caster sugar
4 tbsp golden syrup

115 g (4 oz) plain flour
1 tsp ground ginger
2 tsp brandy

Pre-heat the oven to 175°C (350°F / Gas mark 4). Line two baking sheets with parchment.

Cut the butter into chunks and melt in a saucepan over a gentle heat. Add the sugar and golden syrup and stir until the sugar dissolves. Remove from the heat.

Sift the flour and ginger together and stir into the butter mixture with the brandy.

Drop spoonfuls onto the baking sheets 8 to 10 cm (3 to 4 in) apart. Bake for five to six minutes until golden. Remove the brandy snaps one at a time, and roll them around the handle of a wooden spoon. Twist gently to lift them off the handle. Cool on a wire rack.

Store unfilled in an airtight container for five to seven days.

Makes 2 dozen

vanilla crescents

see variations page 313

Delicate crumbly little cookies that can be served plain or half-dipped in melted chocolate and used to accompany other desserts.

150 g (5 oz) plain flour
115 g (4 oz) unsalted butter
2 tsp vanilla essence

50 g (2 oz) ground almonds
2 tbsp caster sugar
125 g (4½ oz) icing sugar

Pre-heat the oven to 175°C (350°F / Gas mark 4). Line two baking sheets with parchment.

Sift the flour into a bowl and rub in the butter until the mixture resembles fine breadcrumbs. Add the vanilla and stir in the ground almonds and sugar. Work the mixture with your hands until it forms a soft dough.

Roll small pieces of dough into lengths about 1-cm (½-in) thick and 5-cm (2-in) long, and shape into crescents. Bake for 20 minutes, until pale golden in colour.

Remove from the baking sheets and cool on wire racks. Roll each of the crescents in icing sugar.

Store in an airtight container for five to seven days.

Makes 1½ dozen

sugared sablé

see variations page 314

Serve these delicate buttery cookies with soft-textured desserts or enjoy them on their
own with a glass of dessert wine.

450 g (1 lb) plain flour
165 g (5½ oz) icing sugar
300 g (10 oz) unsalted butter

2 tsp vanilla essence
1 egg white
2 tbsp granulated sugar

Grease and flour two baking sheets. Sift the flour and icing sugar together and rub
in the butter.

When the mixture starts to come together, add the vanilla essence. Knead the dough lightly
until smooth. Divide the dough into four and roll into four 4-cm- (1½-in-) wide logs. Wrap
in parchment and refrigerate until firm.

Pre-heat the oven to 190°C (375°F / Gas mark 5). Brush each log with egg white and roll in
the granulated sugar. Cut into 6-mm- (¼-in-) thick slices. Place the cookie slices on the
baking sheets and bake for 8 to 10 minutes. Cool on a wire rack.

Store in an airtight container for five to seven days.

Makes 3½ dozen

brittle cookies

see variations page 315

Enjoy these cookies with chocolate- and coffee-flavoured desserts.

50 g (2 oz) unsalted butter
75 g (3 oz) light brown sugar
2 tbsp golden syrup
1 tbsp instant coffee powder

Grated zest of 1 orange (2 to 3 tsp)
75 g (3 oz) plain flour
75 g (3 oz) toasted flaked hazelnuts

Pre-heat the oven to 175°C (350°F / Gas mark 4). Line two baking sheets with parchment.

Cut the butter into chunks and place in a large saucepan with the sugar and golden syrup. Cook over a gentle heat, stirring until the sugar has dissolved.

Add the instant coffee and orange zest and stir until the coffee powder has dissolved. Remove from the heat and stir in the flour. Drop teaspoonfuls onto the baking sheets 5 cm (2 in) apart and sprinkle with nuts. Bake for 10 to 12 minutes.

Remove from the oven and allow to cool on sheets for one to two minutes before transferring to wire racks to cool.

When completely cool, store in an airtight container for five to seven days.

Makes 2 dozen

florentines

see variations page 316

These delectable nutty cookies are thought to have originated in Florence, Italy.

115 g (4 oz) slivered almonds
25 g (1 oz) chopped red glacé cherries
25 g (1 oz) chopped crystallised lemon and
   orange peel
100 g (3½ oz) butter

100 g (3½ oz) caster sugar
2 tbsp honey
2 tbsp double cream
115 g (4 oz) plain chocolate, chopped
2 tsp safflower oil

Pre-heat the oven to 175°C (350°F / Gas mark 4). Line two baking sheets with parchment. Mix the almonds, glacé cherries and crystallised peel in a bowl and put to one side. Cut the butter into chunks and place in a large saucepan with the sugar and honey. Bring to a boil, stirring occasionally until the mixture thickens slightly. Remove from the heat and stir in the fruit and nuts. Stir in the cream. Allow the mixture to stand for one to two minutes.

Drop spoonfuls of the dough onto the baking sheets 5 cm (2 in) apart. Flatten with the back of a fork dipped in water. Bake for five to seven minutes until golden. Remove from the oven. Using a round cookie cutter, pull the florentines back into shape before they set. Allow to cool completely before removing from the sheet. Melt the chocolate in a heatproof bowl over a saucepan of simmering water and stir in the oil. Dip the undersides of the florentines in chocolate and place them on the parchment. Refrigerate for five minutes to set the chocolate. Once set, store the cookies in an airtight container for five to seven days.

Makes 2 dozen

boules de neige

see variations page 317

Boules de neige, or 'coconut snowballs', are crunchy dessert accompaniments.

3 egg whites	90 g (3¼ oz) flaked coconut
¼ tsp cream of tartar	Pinch of salt
100 g (3½ oz) caster sugar	3 tbsp strawberry jam

Pre-heat the oven to 175°C (350°F / Gas mark 4). Line two baking sheets with parchment.

Whisk the egg whites and cream of tartar. When soft peaks form, add one-third of the sugar. Whisk for a minute and add another third of the sugar. Whisk for a further minute and add the rest of the sugar. Fold the coconut and salt into the meringue.

Use a piping bag and a 1-cm (½-in) nozzle to pipe small rounds 1 cm (½ in) in diameter onto the baking sheets. Bake for 8 to 10 minutes. Transfer the parchment sheets to wire racks. Remove the meringues when cool.

Spread the bases of half the boules de neige with jam and sandwich with the remaining cookie halves. Serve immediately.

Store the unfilled cookies in an airtight container for five to seven days.

Makes 1½ dozen

orange almond tuiles

see variations page 318

These crispy almond cookies are shaped like continental tiles – hence their name, which means 'tile' in French.

100 g (3½ oz) plain flour
125 g (4½ oz) icing sugar
150 g (5 oz) flaked almonds
1 egg

2 egg whites
Grated zest of 1 orange (2 to 3 tsp)
3 tbsp unsalted butter, melted

Pre-heat the oven to 200°C (400°F / Gas mark 6). Grease two baking sheets with butter.

Sift the flour and icing sugar together and stir in the almonds. Add the egg and egg whites to the dry ingredients and stir to combine. Add the orange zest and melted butter.

Spoon walnut-sized amounts of the dough onto the sheets and flatten with the back of a fork dipped in cold water. In order to allow them enough time to assume a shape, bake one sheet at a time. Bake for four to five minutes until pale with a darker golden brown edge. Remove from the oven and shape over a rolling pin.

When completely cool, store in an airtight container for three to four days or in the freezer for three to four weeks.

Makes 3 dozen

almond & lemon cantucci

see variations page 319

Best enjoyed with a glass of after-dinner wine.

2 eggs
150 g (5 oz) caster sugar
150 g (5 oz) whole almonds

Grated zest of 1 lemon (2 to 3 tsp)
250 g (9 oz) plain flour

Pre-heat the oven to 200°C (400°F / Gas mark 6). Grease and flour two baking sheets.

Beat the eggs and sugar together in a large bowl. Add the nuts and lemon zest and mix into the flour to form a stiff paste. Divide the dough in half and shape into two flat loaves about 25 cm (10 in) long and 5 cm (2 in) wide. Bake for 25 to 30 minutes.

Remove from the oven onto a chopping board and slice into thin pieces about 1 cm (½ in) wide using a serrated knife. Reduce the oven temperature to 150°C (300°F / Gas mark 2).

Lay the slices on the two baking sheets and cook for a further 10 to 15 minutes. Turn over each slice and cook for a further 10 to 15 minutes, or until the slices are golden brown. Remove from the oven and allow to cool.

When cool, store in an airtight container. The cantucci will keep for a couple of weeks.

Makes 3 dozen

rum spice cookies

see variations page 320

Spicy rum cookies that taste great served with vanilla ice cream.

200 g (7 oz) rolled oats
225 g (8 oz) plain flour
100 g (3½ oz) coarsely ground almonds
1 tsp ground cinnamon
½ tsp ground allspice
½ tsp ground ginger
1 tsp baking powder

Pinch of salt
225 g (8 oz) unsalted butter
200 g (7 oz) caster sugar
200 g (7 oz) light brown sugar
2 eggs
2 tsp rum flavouring

Pre-heat the oven to 175°C (350°F / Gas mark 4). Line two baking sheets with parchment.

Combine the oats, flour, almonds, spices, baking powder and salt and put to one side.
Beat the butter and sugars until smooth. Add the eggs and rum flavouring and beat until
blended. Stir in the dry ingredients.

Drop spoonfuls of the mixture 4 cm (1½ in) apart on the baking sheets and bake for
12 to 15 minutes. Transfer to a wire rack to cool. Store in an airtight container for five
to seven days.

Makes 3 dozen

lemon wafers

see variations page 321

Crisp lemon wafers are a refreshing accompaniment to ice creams or sorbets.

1 egg
100 g (3½ oz) caster sugar
75 g (3 oz) unsalted butter, melted
Grated zest of 1 lemon (2 to 3 tsp)

Pinch of salt
165 g (5½ oz) plain flour
Pinch of baking powder

Line two baking sheets with parchment. Beat the egg and sugar together in a mixing bowl and stir in the melted butter, lemon zest and salt. Sift the dry ingredients together and stir into the egg mixture. Cover and refrigerate the dough for 30 minutes.

Divide the dough in half. Roll each piece out between two sheets of cling film or parchment to less than 2 mm (¹⁄₁₆ in) thick. Refrigerate until firm. Pre-heat the oven to 200˚C (400˚F / Gas mark 6). Peel the top sheet from the dough and turn upside down. Peel off the second sheet. Use a 6¼-cm (2½-in) cookie cutter and place the cookies 4 cm (1½ in) apart on the baking sheets.

Bake for six to eight minutes. Remove from the oven and lift the parchment to transfer the cookies to wire racks to cool.

When completely cool, store in an airtight container for five to seven days.

Makes 2 dozen

caraway snaps

see variations page 322

Caraway is a wonderful spice – although it is less popular now than it was in the 16th century, when it was widely used to flavour cakes and cookies.

150 g (5 oz) plain flour
150 g (5 oz) icing sugar
3 egg whites

150 g (5 oz) unsalted butter, melted
2 tbsp caraway seeds

Line two baking sheets with parchment. Sift the flour and sugar together. Add the egg whites. Mix until smooth.

Stir in the melted butter and caraway seeds. Refrigerate the paste for 30 minutes.

Pre-heat the oven to 200°C (400°F / Gas mark 6).

Spread the paste in thin rounds about 8 cm (3 in) in diameter onto the baking sheets and bake for four to five minutes until golden. Remove from the baking sheets and shape over a rolling pin or use wine bottles to give a more gradual curve to the cookie.

Store in an airtight container for five to seven days.

Makes 3 dozen

amaretti

see variations page 323

These wonderful Italian cookies are great with coffee, or use them as a base to make Italian-style desserts.

1 tbsp plain flour
115 g (4 oz) icing sugar
190 g (6½ oz) whole lightly toasted
    blanched almonds

3 egg whites
50 g (2 oz) caster sugar
1 tsp grated lemon zest
1 tsp almond essence

Pre-heat the oven to 140°C (275°F / Gas mark 1).

Sift the flour and icing sugar together in a large bowl. Put the almonds in a food processor and blend until ground fine. Add them to the flour and sugar.

In a separate bowl, beat the egg whites to soft peaks and beat in the caster sugar one-third of the amount at a time. Add the lemon zest and almond essence.

Add half of the meringue to the dry ingredients, then carefully add the remaining meringue. Using a piping bag and a 1-cm (½-in) nozzle, pipe the mixture into 4-cm (1½-in) rounds. Bake for 45 to 50 minutes until dry. If the amaretti start to brown, turn the oven temperature down. Remove from the oven and allow to cool. When completely cool, store in an airtight container for one to two weeks.

Makes 2 dozen

variations

langue de chat

see base recipe page 287

langue de chat with chocolate filling
Prepare and bake the basic cookie recipe and make up the chocolate filling as follows: Melt 115 g (4 oz) dark chocolate in a bowl over a pan of simmering water, or in the microwave on a low setting. Boil 4 tablespoons of double cream in a saucepan. Stir the cream into the chocolate until blended. Allow the filling to cool slightly and spread onto the bases of half the cookies. Sandwich with the remaining halves. Store in an airtight container for three to four days.

palets des dames
Prepare the basic cookie dough and pipe small rounds of mixture onto the baking sheets. Put 3 raisins on top of each round and bake.

variations

french macaroons

see base recipe page 289

chocolate macaroons
Prepare the basic cookie dough and substitute 2 tablespoons Dutch process cocoa powder for the pink food colouring. Sandwich the macaroons together with chocolate-hazelnut spread.

mocha macaroons
Prepare the basic cookie dough and substitute 1 tablespoon instant coffee powder for the pink food colouring. Sandwich together with chocolate-hazelnut spread.

lemon macaroons
Prepare the basic cookie dough and substitute yellow food colouring for the pink food colouring. Add the grated zest of 1 lemon (2 to 3 teaspoons). Sandwich the macaroons together with apricot jam or lemon curd.

variations

brandy snaps

see base recipe page 290

cream-filled brandy snaps
Prepare the basic cookie dough and lightly whip 250 ml (8 fl oz) of double
cream. Add 2 tablespoons caster sugar and 1 teaspoon vanilla essence to the
cream. Use a piping bag and a 1 cm (½ in) nozzle to fill the brandy snaps
with cream. Fill each brandy snap from both ends to get an even distribution
of cream.

brandy snap baskets
Prepare the basic cookie dough and shape the warm cookies over small
bowls to make small baskets. Fill with ice cream and fresh fruit for
a quick summertime dessert.

vanilla crescents

see base recipe page 293

lemon crescents
Prepare the basic cookie dough and substitute the grated zest of 1 lemon
(2 to 3 teaspoons) for the vanilla essence.

chocolate-dipped vanilla crescents
Prepare the basic cookie dough and when the cookies are cool, half-dip
them in melted dark chocolate.

hazelnut crescents
Prepare the basic cookie dough and substitute ground hazelnuts for
the ground almonds.

variations

sugared sablé

see base recipe page 294

raisin sablé
Prepare the basic cookie dough and add 75 g (3 oz) raisins to the dough before shaping it into rolls.

walnut and cherry sablé
Prepare the basic cookie dough and substitute 75 g (3 oz) ground walnuts for 75 g (3 oz) cup of the flour. Add 75 g (3 oz) chopped red glacé cherries to the dough before shaping it into rolls.

pistachio sablé
Prepare the basic cookie dough and substitute 75 g (3 oz) ground shelled pistachios for 75 g (3 oz) of the flour. Add 75 g (3 oz) coarsely chopped pistachios to the dough before shaping it into rolls.

variations

brittle cookies

see base recipe page 295

brittle chocolate-orange cookies
Prepare the basic cookie dough and substitute Dutch process cocoa powder
for the instant coffee powder.

lemon vanilla brittle cookies
Prepare the basic cookie dough and substitute 2 teaspoons vanilla essence
for the instant coffee powder and substitute lemon zest for the orange zest.

pistachio brittle cookies
Prepare the basic cookie dough and substitute Dutch process cocoa powder
for the instant coffee powder and pistachios for the hazelnuts.

variations

florentines

see base recipe page 297

ginger florentines
Prepare the basic cookie dough and substitute chopped crystallised ginger for the crystallised peel.

hazelnut & cherry florentines
Prepare the basic cookie dough and substitute coarsely chopped hazelnuts for the almonds and chopped green glacé cherries for the crystallised lemon and orange peel.

variations

boules de neige

see base recipe page 298

chocolate boules de neige
Prepare the basic cookie dough, adding 2 tablespoons sifted cocoa powder to the meringue with the coconut. Sandwich together with chocolate-hazelnut spread.

ginger boules de neige
Prepare the basic cookie dough and add 1 tablespoon finely chopped crystallised ginger to the meringue with the coconut.

variations

orange almond tuiles

see base recipe page 301

coconut tuiles
Prepare the basic cookie dough and substitute 115 g (4 oz) flaked coconut for the almonds.

lemon & almond tuiles
Prepare the basic cookie dough and substitute lemon zest for the orange zest.

hazelnut tuiles
Prepare the basic cookie dough and substitute hazelnuts for the almonds and ½ teaspoon ground cinnamon for the orange zest.

variations

almond & lemon cantucci

see base recipe page 302

rosemary cantucci
Prepare the basic cookie dough and add 2 tablespoons chopped rosemary
to the dough with the nuts and the lemon.

fig & fennel cantucci
Prepare the basic cookie dough, but omit the lemon zest and add
2 teaspoons fennel seeds and 150 g (5 oz) chopped dried figs.

hazelnut & orange cantucci
Prepare the basic cookie dough and substitute toasted hazelnuts for the
almonds and orange zest for the lemon.

variations

rum spice cookies

see base recipe page 303

rum & raisin spice cookies
Prepare the basic cookie dough and add 150 g (5 oz) raisins.

rum, cherry & coconut cookies
Prepare the basic cookie dough and substitute 100 g (3½ oz) flaked coconut for the oats. Add 150 g (5 oz) chopped red glacé cherries.

rum & ginger cookies
Prepare the basic cookie dough and add 4 tablespoons (2 oz) chopped crystallised ginger.

lemon wafers

see base recipe page 304

lemon & poppy seed wafers
Prepare the basic cookie dough and add 1 tablespoon poppy seeds when
adding the dry ingredients.

cinnamon wafers
Prepare the basic cookie dough, but omit the lemon zest and add 1 teaspoon
ground cinnamon when adding the dry ingredients.

spicy wafers
Prepare the basic cookie dough and add 1 teaspoon ground cinnamon,
½ teaspoon ground ginger and ½ teaspoon ground nutmeg when adding
the dry ingredients.

variations

caraway snaps

see base recipe page 307

chocolate caraway snaps
Prepare the basic cookie dough and add 2 tablespoons Dutch process cocoa powder to the dry ingredients.

pistachio snaps
Prepare the basic cookie dough, but omit the caraway seeds and before the cookie dough is baked, sprinkle it with finely chopped pistachio nuts.

lemon & ginger snaps
Prepare the basic cookie dough, but omit the caraway seeds. Add the grated zest of 2 lemons (5 to 6 teaspoons) and ½ teaspoon ground ginger.

variations

amaretti

see base recipe page 308

amaretti with rum

Prepare the basic cookie dough, but omit the lemon zest and almond
essence and add 1 tablespoon dark rum.

cherry amaretti

Prepare the basic cookie dough and add 75 g (3 oz) dried cherries.

soft amaretti

Prepare the basic cookie dough and bake the cookies at 175°C (350°F /
Gas mark 4) for 12 to 15 minutes. When completely cool, store in an
airtight container for five to seven days.

savoury cookies & crackers

Cookies aren't always sweet – perfect with cheese, prepared with herbs, or accompanied by a sweet spread, here are some fabulous savoury cookies and crackers that should not be forgotten. From Scottish oatcakes to blue cheese crumbles and rosemary wafers, this chapter includes all the classics.

triple cheese sandwich cookies

see variations page 344

The ultimate cheesy cookie for those in need of a savoury snack.

75 g (3 oz) mild cheddar cheese, grated
50 g (2 oz) mature cheddar cheese, grated
50 g (2 oz) Parmesan cheese, grated
115 g (4 oz) unsalted butter

150 g (5 oz) plain flour
½ tsp garlic salt
½ tsp paprika
115 g (4 oz) cream cheese

Line two baking sheets with parchment. Blend the cheeses and butter together.

Sift the flour, salt and paprika together and stir into the butter and cheese mixture. Mix to form a soft dough. Shape the mixture into a 4-cm- (1½-in-) thick log. Wrap and refrigerate the dough for 15 minutes until firm.

Pre-heat the oven to 175°C (350°F / Gas mark 4). Cut the dough into 3-mm- (⅛-inch-) thick slices. Place on the baking sheets and bake for 10 to 12 minutes. Transfer to a wire rack to cool. When cool, spread half the cookie bases with cream cheese and then sandwich together with the remaining halves.

Store in an airtight container in the refrigerator for one to two days.

Makes 1½ dozen

cheese & pecan bites

see variations page 345

These savoury cookies are a convenient snack to have on hand and a great base for canapés if you're having a few friends over for a drink.

50 g (2 oz) butter
115 g (4 oz) cheddar, grated
Pinch of cayenne pepper

Pinch of salt
100 g (3½ oz) plain flour
1 cup (5 oz) chopped pecans

Blend the butter and cheese together. Add the pepper, salt and flour and stir to form a smooth dough. Roll into a 5-cm- (2-in-) thick log, wrap and refrigerate the dough for 15 minutes until firm.

Pre-heat the oven to 175°C (350°F / Gas mark 4). Slice the dough into 6-mm- (¼-in-) thick pieces and place on the baking sheets. Press pecans into the tops of each cookie and bake for 10 to 12 minutes until golden.

Transfer to a wire rack to cool. Store the cooled cookies in an airtight container for five to seven days.

Makes 1 dozen

blue cheese crumbles

see variations page 346

Enjoy these cookies on their own or topped with a slice of your favourite cheese.

190 g (6½ oz) wholemeal flour
75 g (3 oz) rolled oats
1 tbsp light brown sugar
1½ tsp baking powder
½ tsp cayenne pepper

¼ tsp salt
115 g (4 oz) unsalted butter
50 g (2 oz) blue cheese
2 to 3 tbsp milk

Pre-heat the oven to 175°C (350°F / Gas mark 4). Line two baking sheets with parchment. Mix all the dry ingredients, except for 2 tablespoons of oats, in a bowl and rub in the butter. Crumble in half the blue cheese and add milk slowly to form a soft dough. Crumble the remaining cheese in a separate bowl and mix with the reserved 2 tablespoons of oats.

Roll out the dough on a lightly floured work surface to 3 mm (⅛ in) thick and cut out rounds using a 6.5-cm (2½-in) cutter. Place the cookies on the baking sheets. Brush the cookies with water and lightly press the reserved cheese and oats on top of the cookies. Bake for 15 to 20 minutes until golden.

Remove from the oven. Place on a wire rack and allow to cool. When completely cool, store in an airtight container for three to four days.

Makes 1 dozen

savoury nut cookies

see variations page 347

You'll simply love these unusual savoury nut cookies – the perfect accompaniment to your after-dinner coffee.

225 g (8 oz) unsalted butter
225 g (8 oz) grated cheddar cheese
300 g (10 oz) plain flour

½ tsp salt
75 g (3 oz) chopped pecans
40 g (1½ oz) crisped rice cereal

Pre-heat the oven to 175°C (350°F / Gas mark 4). Line two baking sheets with parchment.

Mix the butter and cheese together. Stir in the flour and salt and add the pecans and crisped rice cereal. Roll the mixture into small balls and place on the baking sheets. Flatten with the back of a fork dipped in water. Bake for 10 to 12 minutes.

Remove from the oven, transfer to wire racks and cool. Store in an airtight container for three to four days.

Makes 3 dozen

chilli cheese thins

see variations page 348

Hot and spicy wafer-thin cookies are great to nibble while enjoying a pre-dinner drink.

300 g (10 oz) plain flour
½ tsp baking powder
225 g (8 oz) unsalted butter

Pinch of hot chilli powder
115 g (4 oz) Parmesan cheese, finely grated

Pre-heat the oven to 175°C (350°F / Gas mark 4). Line two baking sheets with parchment. Sift the flour and baking powder together and rub in the butter until the mixture resembles breadcrumbs. Then add the chilli powder and Parmesan and continue working the dough until it comes together.

Roll out the dough between two sheets of parchment to less than 2 mm (¹⁄₁₆ in) thick. Remove the top layer of parchment and cut the dough into 10 cm (4 in) lengths 1 cm (½ in) wide. Prick the dough lightly. Re-roll any leftover dough.

Place the cookies on the baking sheets and bake for 8 to 10 minutes until golden. Lift the parchment and transfer to wire racks.

When completely cool, store in an airtight container for five to seven days.

Makes 2 dozen

oatcakes

see variations page 349

These savoury oat biscuits are simple but delicious topped with your favourite savoury spread.

200 g (7 oz) fine oatmeal
¼ tsp bicarbonate of soda
¼ tsp salt

1 tbsp lard
300 ml (10 fl oz) water

Pre-heat the oven to 175°C (350°F / Gas mark 4). Line two baking sheets with parchment.

Mix the oatmeal, bicarbonate of soda and salt together in a bowl. Gently heat the lard and water in a small pan until the lard has melted and add enough of the liquid to make a firm dough.

Roll out the dough onto an oatmeal-covered surface to 3 mm (⅛ in) thick and cut out cookies using a round cutter, or cut into wedges if you prefer.

Place the oatcakes on baking sheets and bake for 12 to 15 minutes. Transfer to a wire rack to cool. Store in an airtight container for five to seven days.

Makes 2 dozen

lemon & black pepper butter biscuits

see variations page 350

Spicy, buttery, melt-in-the-mouth biscuits.

225 g (8 oz) plain flour
115 g (4 oz) unsalted butter
1 tsp grated lemon zest

½ tsp freshly ground black pepper
1 egg
2 tsp rock salt

Pre-heat the oven to 175°C (350°F / Gas mark 4). Line two baking sheets with parchment.

Sift the flour and rub the butter into the flour until the mixture resembles fine breadcrumbs. Add the lemon zest and black pepper and then the egg. Mix to form a stiff dough.

Roll out the dough onto a lightly floured surface to 3 mm (⅛ in) thick. Cut out the dough with a cutter of your choice. Transfer the dough to the baking sheets. Brush with egg white and sprinkle with rock salt.

Bake for 10 minutes or until golden. Cool on a wire rack and store in an airtight container for five to seven days.

Makes 2 dozen

anchovy & olive sticks

see variations page 351

Tip: If the dough of this recipe is too stiff, add water; if it's too wet, simply add flour.

2 tsp dried active yeast
350 ml (12 fl oz) warm water
500 g (1 lb 2 oz) bread flour
2 tsp granulated sugar

1 tsp salt
4 tsp olive oil
3 tbsp chopped anchovies
3 tbsp chopped black olives

Pre-heat the oven to 200°C (400°F / Gas mark 6). Line two baking sheets and sprinkle with semolina. Whisk together the yeast and water and stir in 225 g (8 oz) of the flour and the sugar. Cover and leave in a warm place for 20 minutes. Put the remaining flour in the bowl of a food processor and add the salt, 2 teaspoons olive oil and the starter dough. Mix with the dough hook for 5 to 10 minutes.

Put the dough into a large oiled bowl, brush the top of the dough with 1 teaspoon olive oil and cover with plastic wrap. Leave in a warm place until doubled in size. Flatten the dough on a floured work surface and gently press in anchovies and olives. Roll out the dough with a rolling pin. If the dough shrinks back, cover it with a clean tea towel and allow to rest for 10 minutes. Roll the dough out to 1 cm (½ in) thick and rest it again. Roughly cut the dough into 1 cm (½ in) strips, transfer them to the baking sheets and brush them with the remaining olive oil. Rest them in a warm place for 10 to 15 minutes and then bake for 12 to 15 minutes. They are best eaten on the day they are made.

Makes 2 dozen

rosemary wafers

see variations page 352

Herby little cookies that are great served as an accompaniment to dips or pâté.

300 g (10 oz) plain flour
½ tsp baking powder
Pinch of salt
175 g (6 oz) unsalted butter

75 g (3 oz) Parmesan cheese, finely grated
2 tbsp freshly chopped rosemary
2 egg yolks

Pre-heat the oven to 175°C (350°F / Gas mark 4). Line two baking sheets with parchment. Mix the flour, baking powder and salt together and rub in the butter until the mixture resembles breadcrumbs. Add the Parmesan, rosemary and egg yolks and continue working the dough until it comes together.

Roll out the dough on a lightly floured surface to 3 mm (⅛ in) thick and cut into squares. Place the cookies onto the baking sheets and bake for 8 to 10 minutes until golden.

Lift the parchment and transfer to wire racks. When completely cool, store in an airtight container for five to seven days.

Makes 2 dozen

water biscuits

see variations page 353

Traditional savoury biscuits that are ever so simple to make.

115 g (4 oz) flour
Pinch of salt
2 tbsp water
25 g (1 oz) butter

Pre-heat the oven to 200°C (400°F / Gas mark 6). Line two baking sheets with parchment.

Sift the flour and salt together in a bowl. Put the water and butter in a small pan and heat gently until the butter has melted. Add the liquid to the flour and mix to a smooth dough.

Roll the dough out thinly on a lightly floured work surface. Cut the dough out using an 8-cm (3-in) cutter. Place onto the baking sheets and prick with a fork.

Bake for 12 to 15 minutes until crisp and golden. Cool on a wire rack and store in an airtight container for up to two weeks.

Makes 1½ dozen

mustard & cream cheese sandwich biscuits

see variations page 354

Crispy, crunchy and very addictive, these snack biscuits are a personal favourite.

190 g (6½ oz) plain flour
½ tsp mustard powder
50 g (2 oz) unsalted butter
75 g (3 oz) cheddar cheese, grated

175 g (6 oz) crunchy peanut butter
1 egg
175 g (6 oz) cream cheese

Pre-heat the oven to 175°C (350°F / Gas mark 4). Sift the flour and mustard powder together. Rub in the butter until the mixture resembles breadcrumbs. Stir in the cheese, the add the peanut butter and the egg and mix to a smooth paste.

Roll out the dough on a lightly floured surface to 6 mm (¼ in) thick. Cut out the dough using a 5-cm (2-in) cutter and place the shapes on the baking sheets.

Bake for 10 to 12 minutes until golden. Transfer to a wire rack to cool. Beat the cream cheese to soften it. Spread it on the bases of half the cookies and sandwich together with the remaining cookie halves.

Store in an airtight container in the refrigerator for two to three days.

Makes 2 dozen

twice-baked walnut & raisin finger cookies

see variations page 355

These savoury fruit and nut biscotti are great served with cheese or simply eaten on their own as a late-night snack.

50 g (2 oz) unsalted butter
3 eggs
150 g (5 oz) plain flour
½ tsp baking powder

50 g (2 oz) ground walnuts
50 g (2 oz) cornmeal
150 g (5 oz) raisins
75 g (3 oz) chopped walnuts

Pre-heat the oven to 175°C (350°F / Gas mark 4). Grease and flour two baking sheets. Beat the butter and eggs until well blended. Then add the flour, baking powder, ground walnuts and cornmeal and stir. Add the raisins and chopped walnuts and mix to a smooth paste.

Divide the dough between the baking sheets and shape into two flat loaves about 25 cm (10 in) long and 5 cm (2 in) wide. Bake for 20 minutes until pale golden and dry. Remove from the oven onto a chopping board and slice into thin pieces about 0.5 to 1 cm (¼ to ½ in) wide using a serrated knife. Lay the slices on the baking sheets and cook for a further 10 to 15 minutes, then turn over each slice and cook for a further 10 to 15 minutes or until the slices are golden brown. Remove from the oven and allow to cool. When stored in an airtight container, the cookies will keep for a couple of weeks.

Makes 3 dozen

variations

triple cheese sandwich cookies

see base recipe page 325

triple cheese cookies with blue cheese filling
Prepare the basic cookie recipe. When the cookies are cool, mix 50 g (2 oz) blue cheese with the cream cheese and use to sandwich the cookies together.

walnut-crusted triple cheese cookies
Prepare the basic cookie dough. Before baking the cookies, press 75 g (3 oz) chopped walnuts into the cookie dough. Omit the cream cheese and do not sandwich together.

poppy seed & cheese cookies
Prepare the basic cookie dough, substituting mild cheddar for the mature cheddar and Parmesan cheeses and adding 1 tablespoon poppy seeds to the dough.

variations

cheese & pecan bites

see base recipe page 327

cheese & macadamia cookies
Prepare the basic cookie dough and substitute macadamias for the pecans.

oaty cheese & pecan cookies
Prepare the basic cookie dough and substitute 2 tablespoons oats for
2 tablespoons of the flour.

walnut, cheese & raisin cookies
Prepare the basic cookie dough. Add 50 g (2 oz) raisins to the dough and
substitute walnuts for the pecans.

variations

blue cheese crumbles

see base recipe page 328

blue cheese & pecan crumbles
Prepare the basic cookie dough and substitute 2 tablespoons chopped pecans for 2 tablespoons oats.

blue cheese & raisin crumbles
Prepare the basic cookie dough and add 50 g (2 oz) raisins to the dough after adding the milk.

blue cheese & date crumbles
Prepare the basic cookie dough and add 50 g (2 oz) chopped dates to the dough after adding the milk.

variations

savoury nut cookies

see base recipe page 331

walnut, date & blue cheese cookies
Prepare the basic cookie dough. Substitute blue cheese for half the cheddar, walnuts for the pecans and add 75 g (3 oz) finely chopped dates.

macadamia cookies
Prepare the basic cookie dough and substitute macadamias for the pecans.

mixed nut cookies
Prepare the basic cookie dough. Substitute 75 g (3 oz) chopped peanuts for 15 g (½ oz) crisped rice cereal.

variations

chilli cheese thins

see base recipe page 332

chilli cheese thins with peanuts
Prepare the basic cookie recipe. Before baking, brush the cookies with a little milk and sprinkle with 1 tablespoon chopped peanuts.

double decker cheese thins
Prepare the basic cookie recipe and sandwich the cookies together with cream cheese or peanut butter.

mustard cheese thins
Prepare the basic cookie dough, substituting ¼ teaspoon mustard powder for the chilli powder.

oatcakes

see base recipe page 333

sesame oatcakes
Prepare the basic cookie dough and add 2 tablespoons sesame seeds to
the dry ingredients.

griddled oatcakes
Prepare the basic cookie dough and instead of baking the cookies, cook
them on a griddle pan for six to eight minutes. They will curl up at little at
the edges to give a more uneven appearance.

black pepper oatcakes
Prepare the basic cookie dough and add 2 teaspoons coarsely ground black
pepper to the dry ingredients.

lemon & black pepper butter biscuits

see base recipe page 334

oregano & lemon butter biscuits
Prepare the basic cookie dough and substitute dried oregano for the black pepper.

caraway butter biscuits
Prepare the basic cookie dough. Omit the black pepper and substitute caraway seeds for the rock salt.

sun-dried tomato butter biscuits
Prepare the basic cookie dough. Omit the black pepper and lemon and add 1 tablespoon chopped sun-dried tomatoes to the dough.

anchovy & olive sticks

see base recipe page 337

black & green olive sticks
Prepare the basic cookie dough and substitute green olives for the anchovies.

tomato & rosemary sticks
Prepare the basic cookie dough. Substitute chopped sun-dried tomatoes and chopped fresh rosemary for the anchovies and olives.

parmesan sticks
Prepare the basic cookie dough, omitting the anchovies and olives and adding 75 g (3 oz) finely grated Parmesan to the dough. Sprinkle the sticks with Parmesan after brushing with olive oil.

variations

rosemary wafers

see base recipe page 338

thyme wafers
Prepare the basic cookie dough and substitute thyme for the rosemary.

walnut & rosemary cookies
Prepare the basic cookie dough and substitute 75 g (3 oz) ground walnuts for 75 g (3 oz) of the flour.

goat cheese & rosemary cookies
Prepare the basic cookie dough and substitute 50 g (2 oz) soft goat's cheese for the Parmesan.

variations

water biscuits

see base recipe page 340

bubble biscuits
Prepare the basic cookie recipe. Cut out the biscuits and place them on the baking sheets but do not prick them with a fork. When baked they will bubble.

caraway water biscuits
Prepare the basic cookie recipe. Put the cookies on the baking sheets. After pricking them, brush with water and sprinkle with 1 tablespoon caraway seeds.

salt & pepper water biscuits
Prepare the basic cookie recipe. Put the cookies on the baking sheets. After pricking them, brush with water and sprinkle with rock salt and freshly ground black pepper.

mustard & cream cheese sandwich biscuits

see base recipe page 341

mustard & blue cheese sandwich biscuits

Prepare the basic cookie dough, adding 50 g (2 oz) blue cheese to the cream cheese for the biscuit filling.

mustard, cream cheese & onion sandwich biscuits

Prepare the basic cookie dough, adding 3 finely chopped spring onions to the cream cheese for the biscuit filling.

pecan & cream cheese sandwich biscuits

Prepare the basic cookie dough, omitting the mustard and adding 75 g (3 oz) chopped pecans to the dough.

twice-baked walnut & raisin finger cookies

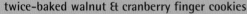

see base recipe page 342

twice-baked walnut & cranberry finger cookies
Prepare the basic cookie dough and substitute dried cranberries for
the raisins.

twice-baked hazelnut & raisin finger cookies
Prepare the basic cookie dough and substitute hazelnuts for the walnuts.

twice-baked walnut & date finger cookies
Prepare the basic cookie dough and substitute chopped dates for the raisins.

index

Almond
amaretti 308, 323
biscotti 20
bites 222
butter cookies 49
and cherry 246, 264
cookies 232
and cranberry 83, 246
cranberry, orange and
almond bars 279
date bars 279
florentines 297
fortune cookies 192
and ginger 275, 277
and lemon cantucci 302
and lemon tuiles 318
linzer cookies 45
macaroons 231, 289, 311
museli seed and nut
bar 195
orange almond
tuiles 301
and pear bars 280
toffee bars 259
alphabet cookies 107, 122
amaretti 308, 323
anchovy and olive
sticks 337
angels, Christmas 182
anzac biscuits 35, 50
apple
apple sauce cookies
211, 225
and apricot bars 223
and cinnamon drops 81
linzer cookies 45
maple apple crumble
cookies 78
and prune bars 208
pumpkin apple
cookies 217
spiced apple muesli
cookies 221
turnovers 87
Viennese pockets
with 82
apricot
and apple bars 223

apricot seed bars 215
bars 216
and coconut 221, 248
flapjack 200
fruit and nut slices 265
and hazelnut chewies 83
and lemon bars 273
and pineapple bars 280

Banana
chocolate banana
fingers 156
and coconut cookies 247
cookies 233
and rum cookies 247
spiced banana
cookies 247
tutti frutti pizza
cookie 114
Beacon Hill cookies 31, 47
bears, gingerbread 99, 117
birthday cookie 174
biscotti 20, 42
black pepper 334, 349, 353
blondies 268, 282
blueberry
and applesauce
cookies 225
berry meringue cookies
239, 251
berry oat bars 212
and cherry bars 216
and chocolate 104
fresh and fruity cookie
cake 190
and lemon 219, 251
and macadamia
cookies 220
neiman marcus berry
cookies 48
tutti frutti pizza
cookie 114
and walnut bars 280
boules de neige 298, 317
brandy snaps 290, 312
brazil nut 83, 252
brittle cookies 295, 315
brownies 257, 274

bubble biscuits 353
butterscotch 250, 282, 284

Candy alphabet cookies 122
cantucci 302, 319
caramel and peanut butter
carnival bars 119
caraway 52, 307, 322,
350, 353
cardamom 216, 224
carnival bars 101, 119
cars, cookie 111, 124
cheese
blue cheese crumbles 328
blue cheese and date
crumbles 346
blue cheese and pecan
crumbles 346
blue cheese and raisin
crumbles 346
chilli cheese thins 332
chilli cheese thins with
peanuts 348
double decker cheese
thins 348
goat's cheese and rosemary
cookies 352
and macadamia
cookies 345
mustard and blue cheese
sandwich biscuits 354
mustard cheese thins 348
mustard, cream cheese
and onion sandwich
biscuits 354
oaty cheese and pecan
cookies 345
parmesan sticks 351
and pecan bites 327
poppy seed and cheese
cookies 344
savoury nut cookies 331
triple cheese cookies with
blue cheese filling 344
triple cheese sandwich
cookies 325
walnut, cheese and raisin
cookies 345

walnut-crusted triple cheese
cookies 344
walnut, date and blue cheese
cookies 347
see also cream cheese
cherry
and almond 246, 264
amaretti 323
anzac biscuits 50
berry meringue cookies 239
berry oat bars 212
and blueberry bars 216
and chocolate 82, 121,
125, 157, 159, 184,
253, 284
and coconut 103, 223,
248, 320
dalmation bars 147
and date bars 283
florentines 297
fruit and nut refrigerator
cookies 91
fruity carnival bars 119
and hazelnut 222, 316
nut brittle squares 275
oat bars 226
oat delights 118
and oatmeal cookies 201
rocky road 53
rum, cherry and coconut
cookies 320
shortbread 249
star cookies 183
toffee bars 276
Viennese pockets with
chocolate and
cherries 82
and walnut 47, 87,
219, 277, 314
chilli cheese thins 332, 348
chocolate
anzac biscuits 50
and apricot flapjack 218
dark chocolate crunchies
243
blondies 268
and blueberry 104
boules de neige 317

brazil nut and chocolate chip
chewies 83
brownies 257, 274
and cherry 121, 125,
157, 159, 253, 284
chewy chocolate cookies
142, 157
chocolate banana fingers 156
chocolate caraway snaps 322
chocolate chip and pecan
crunchies 253
chocolate chip pine nut
bites 87
chocolate chip and raisin
biscotti 42
chocolate cinnamon and
raisin whirls 158
chocolate-dipped
macaroons 120
chocolate-dipped vanilla
crescents 313
chocolate mallow and
strawberry crunchies 121
chocolate mint carnival
bars 119
chocolate mint marbled
cookies 151
chocolate nut and raisin
crunchies 121
chocolate raisin crunchies 253
chocolate raspberry marbled
cookies 151
chocolate-dipped polenta
crescents 84
chocolate-dipped shortbread
fingers 41
and cinnamon 150, 153,
158, 183, 186
and coconut 89, 283
cookie cars 124
cream cheese cookie
slice 266
and cream cheese double
deckers 128, 148
and cream cheese raisin
double deckers 148
and cream cheese walnut
double deckers 148

crystallised lemon
lebkuchen 187
dalmation bars 127, 147
dark-dipped white chocolate
chunk cookies 149
dipped-chocolate
whirls 158
double chocolate Beacon
Hill cookies 47
double chocolate chip
blondies 282
drops 81
Easter nest cookies 165
fingers 141
florentines 297
fortune cookies 192
fruit and nut refrigerator
cookies 91
fudge bars 284
and ginger 132, 152,
153, 158
gumdrop party cookies 193
ice cream cookies 95
langue de chat with
chocolate filling 310
layer bars 237
layered birthday cookie 174
and lemon 79, 150, 155
macaroons 120, 311
mega chocolate fingers 156
millionaire's shortbread
272, 285
mint chocolate ice cream
cookies 115
moccachino cookies 159
neiman marcus ultra
chocolate cookies 48
nut crescents with chocolate-
hazelnut filling 84
oat delights 100
and orange 51, 71, 84, 86,
125, 139, 147, 151, 152,
281, 315
and peanut butter 43, 116
peanut chocolate fingers 156
peanut chocolate mallow
bars 125
and pecan 112, 153, 275, 282

peppermint choc chip
cookies 159
pinwheels 140
and popcorn puffs 227
pretzels 52
shortbread 136, 152,
272, 285
spice cookies 137
toffee bars 259
triple chocolate cookies 146
turtle bars 263, 278
Valentine heart cookies 185
and vanilla 46, 135, 150
Viennese pockets 82
walnut chip cookies 159
whirls 145
white chocolate butterscotch
bars 284
white chocolate chip
toffee bars 276
white chocolate chunk
cookie 131
white chocolate chunk and
pecan cookie 149
white chocolate chunk and
raisin cookie 149
white chocolate fudge
bars 271
white chocolate and
hazelnut tollhouse
cookies 51
white chocolate and
peanut butter
cookies 86
cinnamon
and apple drops 81
and chocolate 86, 150,
153, 158, 183
and lemon butter cookies 49
and pecan meringue nut
cookies 252
shortbread 41
stars 162
wafers 321
coconut
and apricot 221, 248
and banana cookies 247
boules de neige 298

caramel fudge coconut
squares 89
and cherry 103, 223, 248
and chocolate 89, 283
ginger, rum and coconut
cookies 44
jam coconut squares 76
layer bars 237
and pineapple 89, 120, 248
rum, cherry and coconut
cookies 320
and rum squares 89
and sesame seed
cookies 224
tropical bars 269
tuiles 318
wedges 234
wheat and fruit
cookies 229
cranberry
and almond 83, 246
cranberry, orange and
almond bars 279
and macadamia cookies 220
meringues 251
neiman marcus berry
cookies 48
and orange breakfast
bar 215
and peanut butter thumbprints
116
pumpkin cranberry cookies 217
and walnut finger cookies,
twice-baked 355
white chocolate, orange and
cranberry cookies 86
cream cheese
brownies 274
butter sandwich
cookies 68
and chocolate 128,
141, 148, 281
cookie slice 266
fudge nut cookie cream
cheese slice 281
and jam turnovers 80
and lemon-filled cookie
fingers 79

mocha cookie cream cheese
slice 281
and mustard 341, 354
and peanut butter 43
and pecan sandwich
biscuits 354
pizza cookie 92
pumpkin cookies 189
turnover cookies 59
Viennese pockets with
poppy seeds 82
crunchies 104, 121, 243, 253
dairy free shortbread 236, 249
dalmation bars 127, 147
date
and almond bars 279
banana cookies 233
and blue cheese
crumbles 346
fruit and nut slices 265
and pineapple bars 223
sticky date bars 196
tropical bars 269
and walnut 244, 347, 355
wheat and fruit cookies
229
double deckers
alphabet cookies 122
cheese thins 348
cream cheese and chocolate
128, 148
cream cheese raisin and
chocolate 148
cream cheese walnut and
chocolate 148
popcorn 227

Easter chocolate nest cookies
165, 184

Fennel 42, 319
fig 42, 207, 216, 244, 319
flapjack 200, 218
florentines 297, 316
fortune cookies 178, 192
fresh and fruity cookie
cake 190

fruit and nut refrigerator
cookies 91
fruit and nut slices 265
fruity carnival bars 119

Giant pumpkin cookie 173
ginger
and almond 275, 277
boules de neige 317
brandy snaps 290
butter cookies 49
and chocolate 132, 152,
153, 158
crumble cookies 55
crunch refrigerator
cookies 113
extra ginger gingerbread
bears 117
flapjack 218
florentines 316
fortune cookies 192
ginger nuts 24
ginger, rum and coconut
cookies 44
and lemon snaps 322
light ginger nuts 44
maple ginger crumble
cookies 78
melting moments 88
and pear oat bars 226
and pineapple cookies 44
and rum cookies 320
and sesame cookies 224
snicker doodles 46
tropical bars 283
and walnut 44, 78
gingerbread bears 99, 117
goat's cheese and rosemary
cookies 352
golden lebkuchen 187
griddled oatcakes 349
gum drop party cookies
181, 193

Halloween cookies 177, 191
hazelnut
and apricot chewies 83
brittle cookies 295

and cherry 222, 316
chewies 64
crescents 313
crusted lemon bars 273
crusted millionaire's
shortbread 285
fruit and nut refrigerator
cookies 91
macaroons 245
meringue nut cookies 240
nut brittle squares 258
nut crescents with
chocolate--hazelnut filling
84
and orange cantucci 319
pear bars 279
and raisin finger cookies,
twice-baked 355
shortbread 41
toffee bars 276
tuiles 318
Valentine heart cookies 185
Viennese pockets 63
white chocolate fudge
bars 271
and white chocolate
tollhouse cookies 51
honey
almond and ginger honey
nut squares 277
lebkuchen 170, 187
nut bar 215
nut brittle squares 258
nut squares 260
pecan honey nut squares 277
walnut, honey and cherry
squares 277

Ice cream cookies 95, 114, 115

Jam
coconut squares 76
and cream cheese
turnovers 80
drops 60, 81
peanut butter jam
thumbprints 96
jammie dodgers 108

Langues de chat 287, 310
layer bars 237, 250
layered cookie 174, 190
lebkuchen 170, 187
lemon
and almond 302
and almond tuiles 318
and apricot bars 273
bars 255, 273
and black pepper butter
biscuits 334
and blueberry 219, 251
crystallised lemon
lebkuchen 187
and chocolate 79, 150, 155
and cinnamon butter
cookies 49
and cream cheese filled
cookie fingers 79
crescents 313
finger cookies 56
and ginger snaps 322
gumdrop party cookies 193
jammie dodgers 108
lemon vanilla brittle
cookies 315
and lime bars 273
linzer cookies 45
macaroons 311
and oregano butter
biscuits 350
and pine nut 87, 246
and pistachio 42
and poppy seed wafers 321
and raspberry 115, 155
rugelach 188
and spice 79, 124
Valentine heart cookies 185
wafers 304
lemon curd 80, 81
lime and lemon bars 273
linzer cookies 27, 45
lovers' knots 169, 186

Macadamia
anzac biscuits 50
and blueberry cookies 220
and cheese cookies 345

cookies 347
and cranberry cookies 220
dalmation bars 127
honey nut squares 260
meringue nut cookies 252
nut cookies 203
and pineapple chewies 83
macaroons 231
chocolate 120, 311
coconut and cherry 103
coconut and pineapple 120
French 289
hazelnut 245
lemon 311
mocha 311
pistachio 245
walnut 245
malted milk 88
mango bars 269
marshmallow bars 112, 125
maple
apple crumble cookies 78
butter cookies, with pecan
filling 85
chocolate cinnamon maple
cookies 153
coconut wedges 234
fig and walnut bites 207
ginger crumble cookies 78
golden lebkuchen 187
jammie dodgers 108
marbled cookies 135, 151
marshmallow
chocolate mallow and
strawberry crunchies 121
layered cookie 190
mallow bars 112, 125
pizza cookie 114
turtle bars 278
mega chocolate fingers 156
melting moments 75, 88
meringue
berry meringue cookies
239, 251
blueberry and lemon
meringues 251
brazil nut brown sugar
meringue cookies 252

cranberry meringues 251
fresh berry meringues 251
macadamia meringue nut
cookies 252
meringue nut cookies 240
pecan and cinnamon meringue
nut cookies 252
millionaire's shortbread
272, 285
mint
and applesauce cookies 225
and chocolate 115, 119,
151, 159
mixed nut cookies 347
mocha
brownies 274
cookie cream cheese
slice 281
macaroons 311
melting moments 88
pinwheels 155
tollhouse cookies 51
muesli 195, 204, 215, 221
mustard
and blue cheese sandwich
biscuits 354
cheese thins 348
and cream cheese sandwich
biscuits 341
mustard, cream cheese and
onion sandwich biscuits 354

Neiman marcus cookies 32, 48
nut brittle squares 258, 275

Oat delights 100, 118
oatcakes 333, 349
oatmeal
blueberry and lemon
oatmeal cookies 219
and cherry cookies 201
cherry and walnut oatmeal
cookies 219
crescents 84
spiced oatmeal and raisin
cookies 219
oats
banana cookies 233

berry oat bars 212
blue cheese crumbles 328
cherry oat bars 226
coconut wedges 234
museli seed and nut
bar 195
oaty cheese and pecan
cookies 345
pear and ginger oat
bars 226
pineapple and raisin oat
bars 226
olives 337, 351
orange
alphabet cookies 122
butter cookies 85
and caraway pretzels 52
and chocolate 71,
84, 86, 125, 139,
147, 151, 152,
281, 285, 315
and cranberry 215, 279
dalmation bars 147
and hazelnut cantucci 319
lovers' knots 186
marbled cookies 151
orange almond tuiles 301
orange chocolate walnut
mallow bars 125
orange, chocolate, and walnut
tollhouse cookies 51
shortbread 41, 152, 285
white chocolate, orange, and
cranberry cookies 86
oregano and lemon butter
biscuits 350

Palets des dames 310
peach and pecan muesli cookies 221
peanut butter
and caramel carnival
bars 119
and chocolate 43, 86,
116, 125, 156
cookies 23
and cranberry thumbprints 116
and cream cheese 43
flapjack 218

jam thumbprints 96
layer bars 250
oat delights 118
pear
and almond bars 280
and ginger pear bars 226
hazelnut bars 279
pecan
and applesauce cookies 225
brownies 257
and cheese 327, 346
and chocolate 112, 121, 141,
149, 153, 253, 275, 282
and cinnamon meringue nut
cookies 252
and cream cheese sandwich
biscuits 354
fruit and nut slices 265
fudge nut cookie cream
cheese slice 281
fudge pecan refrigerator
cookies 113
honey nut 215, 277
layer bars 237
maple butter cookies with
pecan filling 85
nutty ice cream cookies 115
nutty lebkuchen 187
oaty cheese and pecan
cookies 345
and peach muesli cookies 221
pumpkin pecan cookies 217
and raisin 220, 222
rocky road 40
rugelach 188
savoury nut cookies 331
spiced pecan shortbread 249
totally nuts refrigerator
cookies 113
turtle bars 263
Viennese pockets with
chocolate chips and
pecans 82
wheat and fruit cookies 229
pine nut
bites 72
and chocolate chip bites 87
and lemon 87, 246

pineapple
  and apricot bars 280
  and coconut 89, 120, 248
  and date bars 223
  fruity carnival bars 119
  and ginger cookies 44
  and macadamia chewies 83
  and raisin oat bars 226
  tropical bars 269
pinwheels 140, 155
pistachio
  brittle cookies 315
  and lemon 42
  macaroons 245
  sablé 314
  snaps 322
pizza cookie 92, 114
polenta crescents 67, 84
popcorn puffs 214, 227
poppy seed 82, 321, 344
pretzels 38, 52
prune and apple bars 208
pumpkin cookies 173, 189,
  199, 217

Raisin
  and blue cheese crumbles 346
  and chocolate 42, 121, 148,
    149, 157, 158, 184, 253
  Easter nest cookies 184
  and fig cookies 244
  fruit and nut refrigerator
    cookies 91
  gingerbread bears 117
  and hazelnut finger cookies,
    twice-baked 355
  jam drops 81
  layer bars 250
  muesli cookies 204
  palets des dames 310
  and pecan 220, 222
  and pineapple oat
    bars 226
  pumpkin cookies
    189, 199
  and rum spice cookies 320
  sablé 314
  snicker doodles 46

and spiced oatmeal
    cookies 219
  turnover cookies 59
  and walnut 148, 342, 345
raspberry
  chocolate raspberry marbled
    cookies 151
  fresh and fruity cookie cake
    190
  and lemon 115, 155
refrigerator cookies 91
rocky road 40, 53
rosemary
  cantucci 319
  and goat's cheese cookies 352
  and tomato sticks 351
  wafers 338
  and walnut cookies 352
rugelach 171, 188
rum
  amaretti with 323
  and banana cookies 247
  and coconut squares 44, 89
  and ginger cookies 44, 320
  and raisin spice cookies 320
  rum, cherry and coconut
    cookies 320
  rum spice cookies 303
  Viennese pockets 63
Sablé 294, 314
salt and pepper water biscuits
  353
sesame seed
  apricot seed bars 215
  and cardamom cookies 224
  and coconut cookies 224
  cookies 209
  and ginger cookies 224
  muesli seed and nut bar 195
  oatcakes 349
shortbread
  brown sugar 249
  cherry 249
  chocolate 136, 152, 285
  chocolate and ginger 152
  chocolate and orange 152,
    285
  chocolate-dipped fingers 41

cinnamon 41
  dairy free 236, 249
  hazelnut 41
  millionaire's 272, 285
  orange 41, 152, 285
  Scottish 19
  spiced pecan 249
snicker doodles 28, 46
spice
  apple muesli cookies 221
  banana cookies 247
  Beacon Hill cookies 47
  butter cookies 85
  chocolate pecan spice cookies
    153
  drop cookies 193
  lebkuchen 170, 187
  lemon cookies 79, 124
  oatmeal and raisin cookies
    219
  pecan shortbread 249
  pretzels 52
  pumpkin cookies 189, 199
  rum and raisin spice cookies
    320
  rum spice cookies 303
  wafers 321
stars 162, 183
sticky date bars 196
strawberry
  berry oat bars 212
  chocolate mallow and
    strawberry crunchies 121
  fresh and fruity cookie cake
    190
  rugelach 188
  tutti frutti pizza cookie 114
sun-dried tomato butter biscuits
  350
sunflower seed 195, 215

Thyme wafers 352
toffee bars 259, 276
tollhouse cookies 37, 51
tomato 350, 351
tropical bars 269, 283
tuiles 301, 318
turnover cookies 59, 80

turtle bars 263, 278
twice baked finger cookies
  342, 355

Valentine heart cookies 166, 185
vanilla
  and chocolate 46, 135, 150
  crescents 293
  ice cream cookies 95
  and lemon brittle
    cookies 315
Viennese pockets 63, 82

Wafers
  cinnamon 321
  lemon 304
  lemon and poppy
    seed 321
  rosemary 338
  spicy 321
  thyme 352
walnut
  blondies 268
  and blueberry bars 280
  and cheese 344, 345, 347
  and cherry 47, 51, 87,
    125, 219, 277, 314
  and chocolate 148, 157
  and cranberry finger
    cookies 355
  cream cheese, walnut
    and chocolate double
    deckers 148
  and date 244, 347, 355
  and fig bites 207
  and ginger 44, 78
  macaroons 245
  muesli cookies 204
  nut brittle squares 258
  oat delights 118
  and orange chocolate
    51, 125
  and raisin 342, 345
  and rosemary cookies 352
walnut chip cookies 159
water biscuits 340, 353
wheat and fruit cookies 229
whirls, chocolate 145, 158

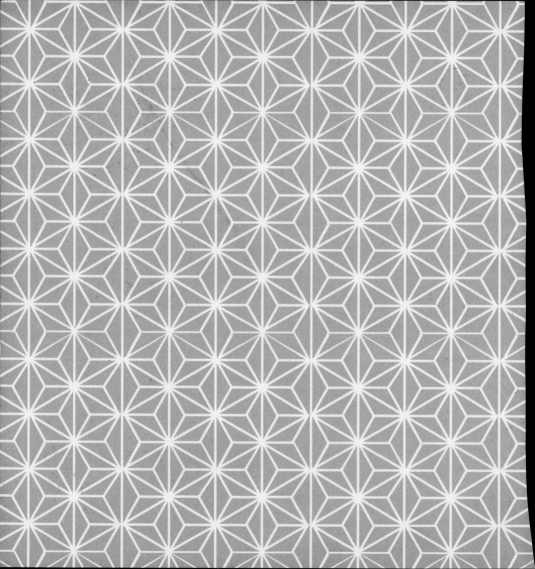